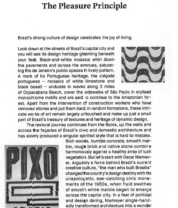
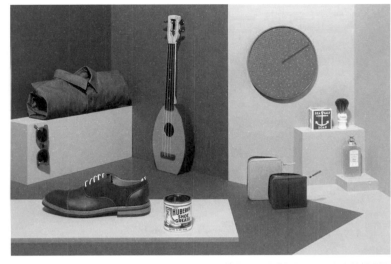

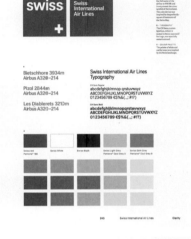

Winkreative Design Stories is a journey through the history of Tyler Brûlé's global design agency. Highlighting a selection of projects from relaunching national carrier Swiss International Air Lines to rebranding Thailand as a magnet for international business, the book spans several continents and an impressive roster of premium clients.
Divided into the core themes of Charm, Craft, Intelligence, Clarity and Storytelling, each chapter of the book showcases a set of projects sharing that characteristic, alongside short, conversational pieces, which offer insight into the thinking and skill behind Winkreative's huge diversity of work, revealing the culture of the agency itself. Still life photography displays Winkreative's unique perspective and distinctive aesthetic sensibility, while comic illustrations and reportage shoots inject a sense of playfulness and bring Winkreative's history and people to life.

Winkreative Design Stories is a warm, understated reference book and design treatise for design influencers and creatives, business figures and policymakers alike, from our unique perspective at the crossroads of commerce and craft.

gestalten
ISBN 978-3-89955-510-3

9 783899 555103

Winkreative
Design Stories

A global view on branding, design and publishing

gestalten

Edited by Winkreative
Proofreading by Transparent Language Solutions
Printed by Optimal Media GmbH, Röbel/Müritz
Made in Germany

Published by Gestalten, Berlin 2014
ISBN 978-3-89955-510-3

© Die Gestalten Verlag GmbH & Co. KG,
Berlin 2014

For more information,
please visit www.gestalten.com.

Bibliographic information published by the
Deutsche Nationalbibliothek. The Deutsche
Nationalbibliothek lists this publication in the
Deutsche Nationalbibliografie; detailed
bibliographic data are available online at
http://dnb.d-nb.de.

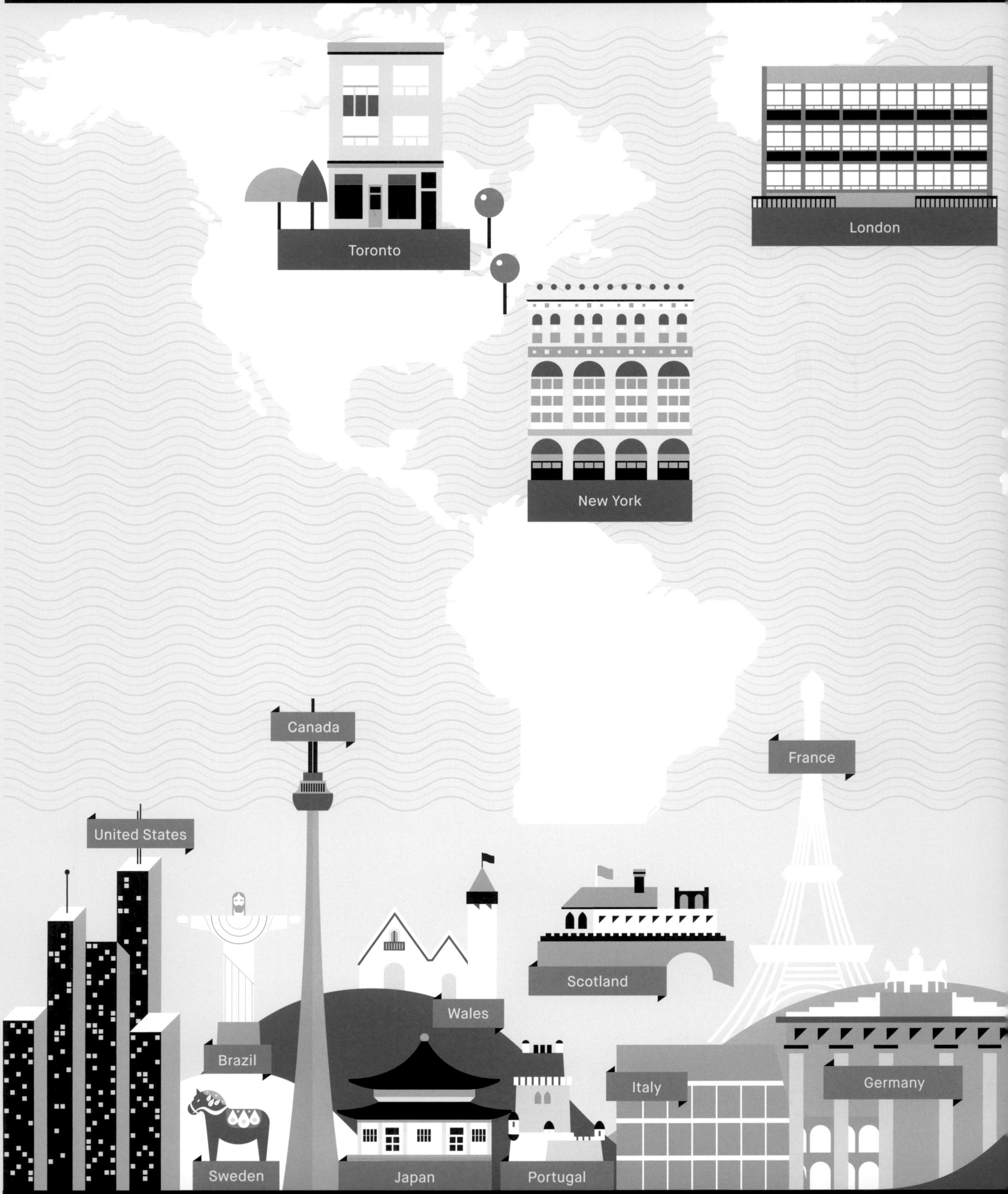

Toronto

London

New York

Canada

France

United States

Scotland

Wales

Brazil

Italy

Germany

Sweden

Japan

Portugal

Contents

Tyler Brûlé
CEO and founder
of Winkreative

This is a short story about broom closets, full circles, international talent, inspiring clients and a tireless commitment to raising the bar.

In 1998, in an office high above the Thames at Waterloo bridge, the publishing team at *Wallpaper* magazine was given the unique opportunity to expand beyond its core publishing business and launch a new division devoted to developing new brands, editorial projects, packaging and environments. Although the magazine was already stretched for space, a small broom and mop cupboard beside the reception desk was refitted with three desks and turned into the first office for a company we dubbed Wink. With two designers and a handful of accounts to kick things off, it wasn't long before the tiny agency demanded more resources, expanding to another floor and adding more designers, writers, editors and project managers to the mix. Shortly after a desk was installed in New York, the client roster was enhanced by larger publishing projects, and by 2001 Wink had begun the process of breaking away from *Wallpaper* and its parent company, Time Inc. Come spring 2002, Winkreative was the name on the plaque hanging above our new headquarters in a cosy corner of Zurich, and a fleet of Airbuses with our fresh logo for national carrier Swiss International Air Lines were taking off from and touching down at airports around the world. Something of a breakthrough project for the agency, the work for Swiss allowed us to indulge a few of our childhood dreams (painting big things that actually flew, launching CDs, designing uniforms) and also move into new areas of expertise.

At the core of our business has always been the belief that every project must be considered in terms of how it will play out on the printed page (or screen) when retold by journalists and columnists, whether they're writing about a new financial services brand, a relaunched athletic footwear business or a new supplement for a daily newspaper.

Winkreative functions much more like a newsroom than a traditional creative agency. Fed by a network of correspondents and contributors around the world, our offices are as much in the business of newsgathering and analysis as they are centres for project management and business development. Now numbering 50 staff from more than 20 countries, we share space with our sister *Monocle* magazine at our operational headquarters in London's Marylebone and have recently expanded our reach to working on national brands along with more traditional consumer projects. At press time, we had just completed a new round of work for the Government of Thailand and a flagship rail project for the city of Toronto. Over the next 344 pages, you'll see a host of projects that define not only our style but also how we've worked with clients to overcome complex challenges – often on the tightest of deadlines. To date, we're still looking forward to overhauling a full department store, branding a cruise ship company, tackling a subway system (stations, railcars, kiosks – the lot) and launching a sunny little beach club at the eastern end of the Mediterranean. If you own any of these and need a new coat of paint (or even a strategy), we look forward to hosting you.

To all our clients and collaborators, thank you for your support.

Storytelling

Storytelling is why Winkreative started – to tell the story behind the brand. It's not just the championing of an end product, place or service; it's about conveying the ideas, processes and experiences behind what elevates a brand into something more. We identify a way to tell the story, to capture the essence of a brand and translate it in a way that is right and just. The vast wilderness and future visions of São Lourenço do Barrocal cannot be confined to two-dimensional design, Louis Vuitton's rich travel heritage has to be experiential and the colourful history of Hermès deserves a super-modern celebration. Whatever the story, our work is not only the output of materials. It's the beginning, the middle and the end – the whole story.

Pride of Place

Winkreative has worked with São Lourenço do Barrocal since 2004 capturing the essence of this unique development. Owner José António Uva describes balancing modern architecture with the preservation of the landscape.

Set in Portugal's wild and beautiful Alentejo region, São Lourenço do Barrocal is a new vision for modern country living. Working with a vast landscape that has been in his family for 200 years, José António Uva is using the site's historical elements to build a modern community.

Winkreative
How would you describe Barrocal for those who don't know it?

José
It's definitely a modern countryside retreat. It's set within an estate that has been in our family for 200 years, producing wine, olive oil, vegetables. On the one hand, it's still very much a safe world – one of the most preserved, most beautiful and least populated landscapes in western Europe. But on the other hand it's not lost in time. It's contemporary in that we're embracing modern culture. That's not the same thing as saying it's a globalised project. It's very much centred on local culture, but it's modern in terms of modern living.

Winkreative
What is unique about it?

José
There are two things. One is the aesthetic side of it, the sense of beauty, the vastness of the landscape, the colours, the architecture both old and new, and the food. This is all very much an aesthetic experience. On the other side is the geography – the Alentejo, which is one-third of the country but only has one-tenth of its population, and is secluded in a very special way. It's very well preserved and has an enormous coastline and an inland wine region, but is still within easy reach of cities like Lisbon. These are the two sides of the uniqueness – the beauty of the region and the proximity to European destinations.

Winkreative
What does "modern country living" mean?

José
Well, this is interesting. Country life is mostly still regarded as a conservative and old-fashioned way of life, and, while there is absolutely nothing wrong with that, in most cases the architecture, the food and even the hospitality can become a pastiche of bygone eras. There is this idea that countryside should be rustic, and often the result is a certain fakeness or make-believe, which is a discredit to what can be genuine. We wanted to change this perception, at least here, and make the conservation of a place, the architecture and the way of life a part of the process. However, there is the question of suitability – suiting a building for the purpose of its contemporary use. In our case it's transforming old buildings to suit a new purpose but in such a way that the buildings remain true to their old selves and have a new life and use. So modern country living is about connectivity, obviously, but it's also about changing the perception that country life needs to be old-fashioned and the local history forgotten.

Winkreative
What role do heritage, family and local community play at Barrocal?

José
There is definitely a sense of family legacy and continuity. My main interest is to open that legacy to others, to create a broader and more diverse community of people who can come and build their own attachments and legacies while being part of this community. Above all, I want Barrocal to be a place where everyone can have a sense of ownership and belonging.

Winkreative
You must feel a huge emotional attachment to the site. How do you balance the family enjoyment with the commercial aspect?

José
The balance is actually quite easy to maintain, as it's really the thing that drives me. For example, if we can build a community where my nine-month-old son is able to make friends and share experiences with other kids, then we've done something right.

Winkreative
What is it about Barrocal that attracts such eminent architects as John Pawson and Eduardo Souto de Moura?

José
There are two things. One is more technical and has to do with the landscape architect João Gomes da Silva, who invested an enormous amount of time and effort into understanding the various layers of history and memory of this landscape to ensure that the estate will remain agriculturally the same, and that there is a symbiosis between the new architecture and the existing elements. There's a lot of groundwork done, a common language created, so the architect can connect very easily with the work so far. On a more bucolic side, Barrocal is an agricultural patchwork of

land, covered with Neolithic stones and century-old olive trees, and I think the architects identify very much with a landscape where they have these historical and agricultural references. It's very much how they engage with the project.

Winkreative
How do you ensure the development won't compromise the well-being of the land and environment?

José
There is a strict legal framework. With time, most developments misrepresent what they once stood for, and the ones that work remain loyal to their principles and environment. The Sea Ranch in northern California is a great example and has been a real model for us. I've been there quite often, and it still follows the principles it started with in the 1960s. One of the founding architects says the secret to the continuity of the project is a very strict legal structure, and that's what we tried to make here. Coming in, architects, buyers, everyone will know what these are. We want to make sure the whole estate is more relevant than the sum of its parts.

Winkreative
How branded should an environment be? Can you strike a balance between articulating a space and just letting it be?

As architects and landscapers, I think we have a tendency to overdesign, overbuild and excessively occupy the landscape.

José
As architects and landscapers, I think we do have a tendency to overdesign, overbuild and excessively occupy the landscape – to do too much. Developers have been doing the most dreadful work in all European countries for years, both on the coast and in the countryside, so there's a bad reputation. Our principles are set from the beginning; the over-multiplying is where you go wrong, so there's a level of self-restraint that we make sure we have, an effort to be concise, which I think is important. My role is more or less to make sure that the interaction between the architect and the designer does not dilute the intrinsic value of the place.

Winkreative
What does authenticity mean to you?

José
Well I'm thinking more in terms of place. For me, authenticity reflects the culture of the people who inhabit that place, both past and present. The reality is that authenticity can be aesthetically quite unappealing or quite beautiful; here, we're fortunate that the people who inherited this place passed along a beautiful legacy, and it's now in our hands to enrich further.

Winkreative
What were you looking for from Winkreative?

José
When we first spoke to Winkreative, we already had an initial concept for the development. After long conversations, dinners and walks around the countryside, it was pretty clear that we shared the same aesthetic and ideas. We asked if it was possible to build a picture of what's being done here, and that's what really impressed me in the beginning: the way that Winkreative was able to communicate the ideas through beautiful work. It made coming together very easy.

Winkreative
In what ways has Winkreative captured the essence of Barrocal?

José
Not many people know this place. If you're talking about Tuscany, everybody has an idea of what it's like, so the interesting thing here is that we really have a chance to understand our own aesthetic, but also the Alentejo, and to a larger extent, southern Iberian culture. That ended up taking up a large part of the narrative. The films, for example, are trying to portray not only the project but also the cultural context of the region, which makes the whole thing more interesting. It's so much bigger than the project itself.

Winkreative
How has the work changed the business?

José
Wink really identified this larger scale – the region and the importance of representing that. In that sense, Wink has changed our perception of who we are and really laid the foundations of our business. Filming together for almost 10 days straight made me see things through fresh eyes. The inspiration was mutual, so the work is always surprising.

Winkreative
What's your aim? What's next? What does the future hold for Barrocal?

José
The funny thing is, there's so much I can do as a developer, but there is a point where the role to be played is by the people who come and inhabit this place. The same goes for the agricultural work we do. It's about the people who help us make the wine, the olive oil – there's a new ecosystem around the property that's growing organically, and it will continue to take on a life of its own. That's our aim: for Barrocal to be this open space that, thanks to the input of all these different people, will surprise us beyond all our expectations.

São Lourenço do Barrocal

Country
Portugal

Work
Strategy
Identity
Publishing
Digital design
Packaging
Animation
Film

São Lourenço do Barrocal and Winkreative have been working together since 2004, bringing to life this softly spoken, thoughtfully planned development of a seventh-generation family estate in Portugal's Alentejo region.

The culmination of many meetings in picturesque settings, unparalleled local hospitality and several years of work is the Winkreative-designed website, which features a series of films exploring the estate and region, as well as stunning animations revealing plans from the award-winning architects involved in the project. Winkreative also designed labels for the estate-bottled wine and a book showing São Lourenço do Barrocal's remarkable vision.

A, NEXT PAGES –
PHOTOGRAPHY
Photography of the region.

A

São Lourenço do Barrocal

A – IDENTITY
Research showed that São Lourenço do Barrocal is the historic name of the site.

B – COVER, SPREAD
The book contains two paper stocks: a richly textured matte stock dedicated to pages telling the story of the site's heritage, and a complementary semi-matte for pages relating to the future plans of the project. The contents page includes typographic references to Portuguese history and culture, while drawings illustrate the stories of small producers based in the area.

C – SPREADS
The heritage of the site is central to everything at Barrocal. The book includes a carefully researched and considered history of the region, to ensure this knowledge is passed on and to protect the integrity of the site.

B

c

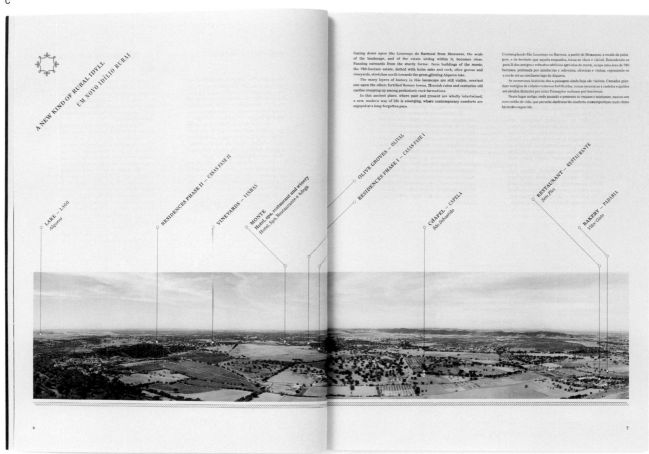

A NEW KIND OF RURAL IDYLL
UM NOVO IDÍLIO RURAL

LAKE — LAGO
Alqueva

RESIDENCES PHASE II — CASAS FASE II

VINEYARDS — VINHAS

MONTE
Hotel, spa, restaurant and winery
Hotel, spa, Restaurante e Adega

RESIDENCES PHASE I — CASAS FASE I

OLIVE GROVES — OLIVAL

CHAPEL — CAPELA
São Sebastião

RESTAURANT — RESTAURANTE
Sem fim

BAKERY — PADARIA
Vítor Gaio

Gazing down upon São Lourenço do Barrocal from Monsaraz, the scale of the landscape, and of the estate sitting within it, becomes clear. Fanning outwards from the sturdy forms: farm buildings of the monte, the 780-hectare estate, dotted with holm oaks and cork, olive groves and vineyards, stretches north towards the great glinting Alqueva lake.

The many layers of history in this landscape are still visible, overlaid one upon the other: fortified Roman towns, Moorish ruins and centuries-old castles cropping up among prehistoric rock formations.

In this ancient place, where past and present are wholly intertwined, a new, modern way of life is emerging, where contemporary comforts are enjoyed at a long-forgotten pace.

Contemplando São Lourenço do Barrocal, a partir de Monsaraz, a escala da paisagem, e da herdade que aquela empadra, torna-se clara e visível. Estendendo-se para lá dos antigos e robustos edifícios agrícolas do monte, ocupa uma área de 780 hectares, pontuada por azinheiras e sobreiros, oliveiras e vinhas, espraiando-se a norte até ao cintilante lago do Alqueva.

As numerosas histórias desta paisagem ainda hoje são visíveis. Camadas guardam vestígios de cidades romanas fortificadas, ruínas mouriscas e castelos erguidos em séculos distantes por entre formação rochosa pré-histórica.

Neste lugar antigo, onde passado e presente se cruzam e misturam, nasce um novo estilo de vida, que permite desfrutar do conforto contemporâneo num ritmo há muito esquecido.

A YEAR AT BARROCAL
UM ANO NO BARROCAL

For all its easy accessibility from Lisbon and Évora, central Alentejo remains one of Europe's great undiscovered landscapes. This ancient terrain, with its medieval towns and sleepy villages whose ways of life have hardly changed in centuries, still retains a wonderful sense of connection to the land and to the rhythms of the year. In this magnificent landscape it is nature that holds sway: the jewel-like carpets of wildflowers that clothe a very meadow in spring, the thousands of cork and oak trees whose dark leaves shelter wild-roaming pigs and birds, and, at night, the vast velvet blackness of the arching sky, scattered with millions of stars.

O Alentejo Central, apesar do fácil acesso desde Lisboa e Évora, permanece uma das mais belas paisagens por descobrir na Europa. Esta terra antiga, com cidades medievais e aldeias adormecidas, cujo estilo de vida pouco mudou ao longo dos séculos, emana uma forte sensação de comunhão com a terra, moldada pelo ritmo das estações do ano. Nesta magnífica paisagem a natureza é rainha: os campos floridos qual jóias esculpidas cobrem os campos na Primavera, os milhares de sobreiros e azinheiras oferecem abrigo e sombra às aves e aos porcos selvagens, e, à noite, o céu cobre a terra de um veludo negro pontuado por milhões de estrelas cintilantes.

A

A – WEBSITE
The website includes interviews with the architects and provides insight into every facet of the project, including maps and plans, models, film and a daily journal.

B – FILM
Film is an effective way to capture the vast landscape. A series of films documents the estate, giving the perspectives of the family and architects involved in the project.

B

The Original Adventurer

For the past 160 years, Louis Vuitton has been designing inventive objects, from cases for trips to Mars to trunk beds taken to the Congo. Today, that spirit continues.

Louis Vuitton started with an adventure. In 1834, at the tender age of 13, Louis set off from his native Jura Mountains for Paris. By 1837, he was padding through the grime and filth, luxury and grandeur of France's capital to the district of La Madeleine – an area brimming with innovation and enterprise – just short of the swish Saint-Honoré, which would later become his home.

Louis showed unparalleled skill as an apprentice box-maker (a rich artisanal industry with specialised techniques, not unlike master carpentry) and meticulously crafted wooden trunks specially ordered by customers, each one designed around the objects it would contain. Great precison was required to build

compartments tight enough to hold even the smallest treasures in place against the bumpy roads and the rough handling of horse-drawn carriages.

Established in 1854, Maison Louis Vuitton opened to immediate success thanks to Louis's invention of the first flat trunk – an ingenious, elegant and strong model that symbolised the birth of modern luggage. A legend was born, and as the industrial age dawned, travel became accessible, offering the possibility of discovery.

Nineteenth-century trunk commissions belonged to the explorers and adventurers. With colonial expansion across the globe, expedition specifications ranged from the everyday

to the utterly obscure: copper-coated with picnic pouches in 1903, trunk beds taken to the Congo in 1905, the unsinkable Aero trunk of 1920 – watertight with added buoyancy should your newfangled flying machine unexpectedly fall from the sky – and specially shaped, stackable Citroën car trunks for the exotically named Yellow and Black expeditions from Paris to Beijing and Timbuktu in 1924.

But leave it to the royals to really ramp things up. Louis Vuitton luggage was made for anything from cigars to cocktails, croquet to Christmas decorations, watches to watercolours, music to magic, toiletries to tennis rackets – imagine the wildest whim and the Louis Vuitton workshop has surely enclosed it in a snug pocket of red velvet. In 2004, to celebrate the 150th anniversary of the Louis Vuitton company, an invention competition revealed a portable shower trunk, the ultimate birthday-cake box and the famous Mars trunk, a resin-clad, egg-shaped lifeline designed to be shot into space.

Louis Vuitton continues to hand craft equipment for our wild world. Contemporary commissions read like an anthropological study of modern culture: personalised and mono-grammed (obviously) for computers, iPods, skateboards, PlayStations, solar panels, flat-screen TVs and even animals, courtesy of Marc Jacobs in 2009.

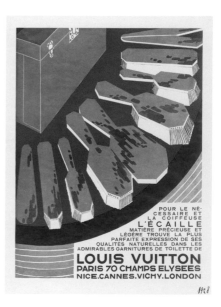

A Louis Vuitton product is a true symbol of craftsmanship and industry, practicality and innovation, pragmatism and romanticism, quality and functionality – another utilitarian object made with the same love, care and attention to detail is hard to find. Few objects adapt to modern culture and maintain their historical integrity in quite the same way.

PREVIOUS PAGE
Illustration of a classic Louis Vuitton desk trunk from 1926.

TOP AND RIGHT
Illustration of the open view of the camp bed from 1905; advertisement from *Vogue*, 1928.

Louis Vuitton

Country
France

Work
Strategy
Publishing
Environment

To celebrate Louis Vuitton's expert authority on travel and its historical sense of adventure, Winkreative created L'Aventure – a unique pop-up retail experience on Paris's legendary Avenue Montaigne. Distinctively designed to take visitors to a faraway place, L'Aventure showcases Louis Vuitton's comprehensive luggage collection as well as its unique packing and personalisation services.

Created for the 21st-century traveller, L'Aventure brings Louis Vuitton's

unique heritage and unbeatable craftsmanship to a modern, globe-trotting audience.

In support, Winkreative conceived the postcard series – a portable A-Z of the most deluxe and diverse destinations around the globe. Additionally, featuring evocative photography and illustration, the Winkreative-designed *L'Aventure* journal showcases Louis Vuitton's specialist travel services – what to pack, how to pack it and where to go. Let the adventure begin.

A – PHOTOGRAPHY
The journal includes an "Art of Packing" photo shoot.

NEXT PAGE – MAP
World map custom-designed for L'Aventure.

A

AUCKLAND / AUCKLAND

NOUVELLE-ZÉLANDE / NEW ZEALAND

LOUIS VUITTON

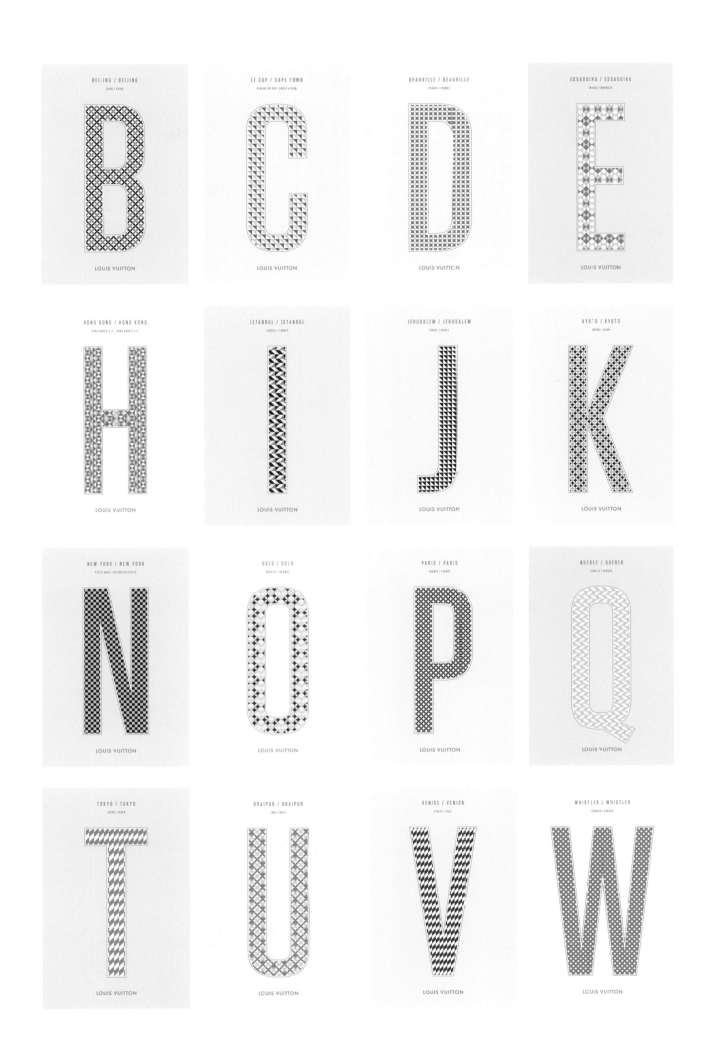

PREVIOUS PAGE –
A-Z CARDS
The pattern on each
letter is unique, inspired
by the Louis Vuitton
motif and designed to
reflect the character of
the city it represents.

A – LOGO

B – SPREAD
The journal continues the
A-Z template, listing the
highlights of each city.

C – SLIP CASE
Designed to hold
the collectible A-Z
card series, the
slipcase resembles
a passport holder.

D – JOURNAL
The canvas cover comes
in three shades and is
gold foil blocked.

OPPOSITE AND
NEXT PAGE –
PHOTOGRAPHY
The "Art of Packing"
photo shoot.

A

B

C

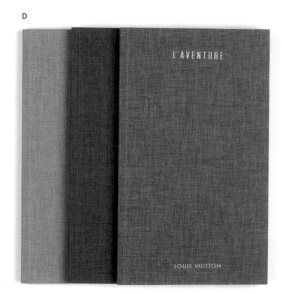

D

A – POP-UP SHOP
A corner library featured a curated assortment of travel objects, books and magazines from all over the world.

B – FEATURE WALL
The clad ceiling and plants create a sub tropical interior. The hand-painted wall is an artistic take on Louis Vuitton's personalisation services.

C – POSTERS
The specially commissioned graphic city illustrations are a contemporary twist on vintage travel posters.

NEXT PAGE – ANIMATION
The animation is a fantasy piece based on the design of the signature Louis Vuitton monogram.

B

THE ADVENTURES OF THE MONOGRAM
by LOUIS VUITTON

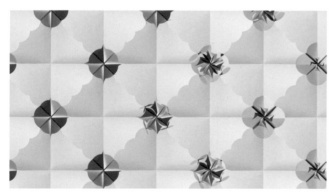

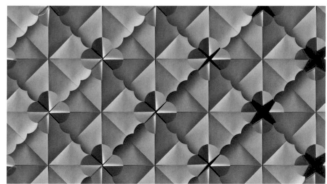

Storytelling takes us far and wide, from the manicured lawns of London via the natural wonders of Taiwan to the bustling streets of Fukuoka.

Projects
**Wimbledon | Sirin Airport | Rhone
Isaora | Taiwan Tourism Bureau
Fukuoka City**

Client
Wimbledon

Country
United Kingdom

Work
Publishing

A debenture for Centre Court at Wimbledon is the ultimate indulgence for any tennis fan. Just like the debenture itself, Winkreative's Centre Court and No.1 Court books take the holder closer to the action, communicating the uniquely elegant thrill of a day at Wimbledon. Conceived, written, photographed and art-directed by Winkreative, the books have a layout and finish that conveys pure prestige, while the narrative brings to life the muscle and magic of the world's oldest tennis championships.

Work is currently under way for the next Centre Court debenture book.

A

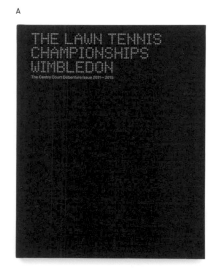

B

A – COVER
The cover and headline font of the 2011-15 Centre Court debenture book was inspired by the Wimbledon scoreboard.

B – BOOK
Created to promote the five-year debenture tickets for Centre Court, the book is split into two parts – history and photography, and financial information.

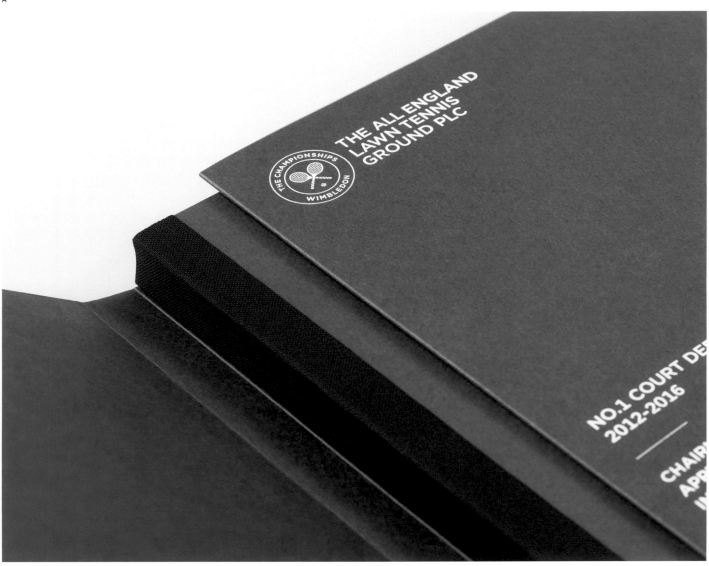

PREVIOUS PAGES –
PHOTOGRAPHY
Winkreative
commissioned and art-
directed photography
to work alongside
Wimbledon's archive of
sports photography.

A – COVER
The 2012-16 No.1 Court
debenture book is
Swiss-bound, and its
cover is screen-printed.

Client
Sirin Airport

Country
Russia

Work
**Strategy
Identity
Publishing**

Sirin will be a new international airport dedicated exclusively to private aviation. Based in Moscow, the airport will offer a personal, tailored service, as well as luxury amenities such as a hotel and restaurant.

When establishing a name and identity, Winkreative drew on the Sirin, a mythical creature from Russian folklore that is half-woman,

half-bird. The visual identity and logo convey the grace, elegance and sense of flight associated with this historical legend.

Winkreative designed a book to support the ambitions of this proudly Russian yet cosmopolitan project.

A

SIRIN
AIRPORT MOSCOW

A – LOGO
Derived from aeroplane wings, the arrows face both east and west, suggesting dynamism and international travel.

A

B

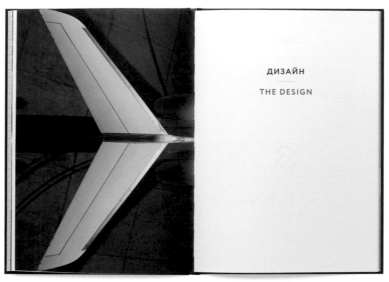

ДИЗАЙН

THE DESIGN

A – BOOK
The logo on the cover
is foil blocked in black
and copper and sits in
a linen covered box.

B – SPREADS
Illustration, architectural
renders and large-scale
photography convey
the confident vision of
Sirin Airport.

OPPOSITE – PATTERN
The pattern is
constructed using the
marque. The colour
palette is built around
ice blue and a warm
copper tone.

Client
Rhone

Country
Switzerland

Work
Identity
Advertising

Rhone is a Swiss company with international operations, offering a comprehensive range of financial-planning services. Winkreative was commissioned to develop a corporate identity, a series of brochures and stationery and an advertising campaign, all based on the concept that structure is fundamental to successful wealth planning.

A

A, NEXT PAGES –
ADVERTISING
Bringing order to chaos: in the Rhone advertising posters, structure is given to areas that are often disorganised, such as the kitchen, the garden shed and the playroom.

COMPLEXITY CONFUSES.
CLARITY INSPIRES.

Structure is fundamental to successful wealth planning. We can help you make the right choices. Our global experts will set up your wealth in forms that safeguard your assets, optimise your financial affairs and meet the needs of your family.

Life isn't always structured. But we are.

Rhône
rhoneservices.com

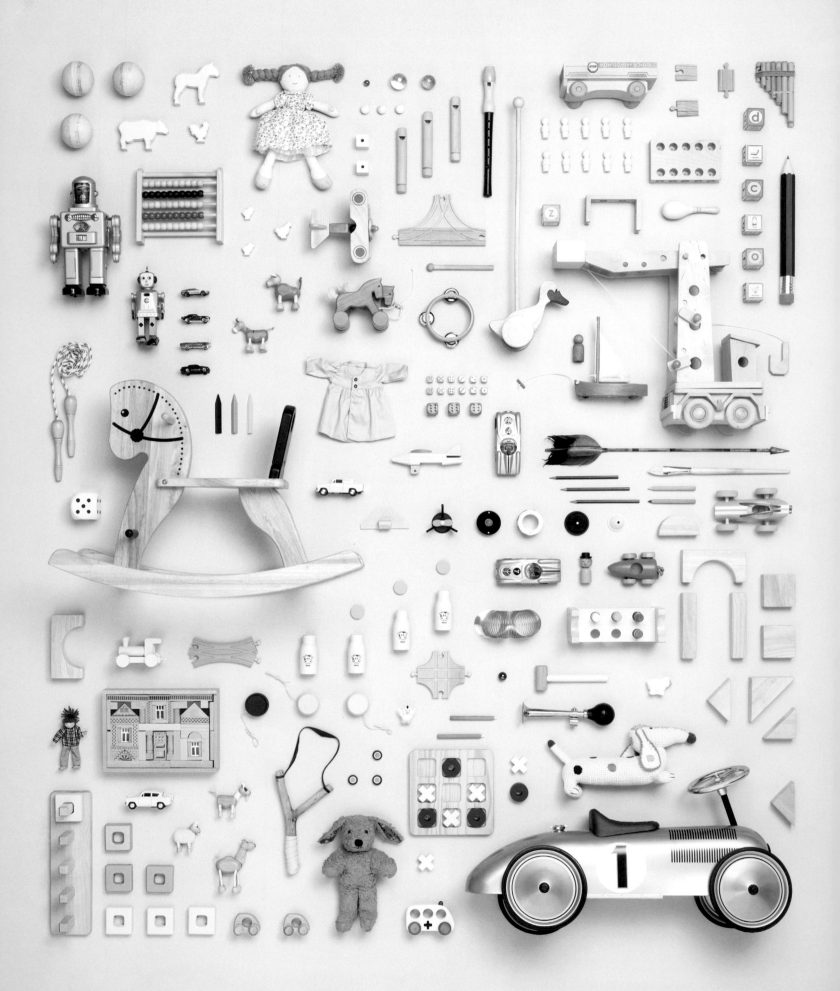

Client
Isaora

Country
United States

Work
**Identity
Publishing
Digital design**

Isaora is a New York-based fashion brand founded on the belief that premium performance and progressive style need not be mutually exclusive. Utilising advanced material technology and state-of-the-art construction, Isaora combines the functional benefits of high-performance technical apparel with a progressive, fashion-forward aesthetic.

As an emerging brand, Isaora needed a strong visual direction that represented its dedication to high-performance winter wear and a modern, urban aesthetic. Winkreative designed the company's identity, look book and stationery, and provided art direction for photography. The stylish Wink-designed website highlights Isaora's refusal to sacrifice style for performance.

A

B

ISA ORA ®

A – SYMBOL
The snowflake is drawn from the sloped edge of the letter A within the logotype.

B – LOGOTYPE
A simple expression of both the modern, high-performance character of the brand and the mountains that inspire it.

NEXT PAGES –
PHOTOGRAPHY AND MAGAZINE
The broadsheet magazine juxtaposes the element of extreme sport with studio fashion shoots. The monochrome theme aligns with Isaora's first collection and tells the story behind key fabrics.

WHETHER YOU LEAVE TWO TRACKS IN THE SNOW OR ONE, WHETHER YOU CONFRONT THE ELEMENTS ON ALASKA'S CHUGACH STEEPS OR A DRIVING RAINSTORM IN MANHATTAN, ISAORA PROVIDES STYLE, PERFORMANCE, AND PROTECTION — WHEREVER YOUR ADVENTURE TAKES YOU.

MENS CLOUD CAMO 2-L PCM JACKET
Dual-tone, relieved, technical double-insulated hooded jacket with PrimaLoft™One and schoeller® Phase Change Materials.
Style No. 91633

ESTRELLA AROPAK JACKET
Iridescent 2-layer anorak performance jacket.
Style No. 91494 (Fabric: Wax)

Client
Taiwan Tourism Bureau

Country
Taiwan

Work
Strategy
Identity
Advertising
Animation

To raise awareness and consideration of Taiwan as a destination for long-distance travellers, the Taiwan Tourism Bureau asked Winkreative to develop a compelling global advertising campaign highlighting the country's special appeal.

Given its geographical location and famously warm welcome, we positioned Taiwan as the "Heart of Asia". In addition to a new modern logo and identity, a dynamic

illustrated heart encapsulates an ever-changing selection of Taiwan's many attractions, while distinctive saturated photography was used as destination advertising for the Taiwan Tourism Bureau.

Exploring some of the country's lesser-known charms in categories ranging from nature to culture and food, the advertising campaign ran in high-profile national and international titles.

A

A – ILLUSTRATION
The lead visual device tells the story of Taiwan's ever-changing culture.

Taiwan

THE HEART OF ASIA

The shapes within the stencilled logo present key cultural elements of the progressive and forward-thinking country.

C – ILLUSTRATIONS
Using illustration helps communicate the diversity of Taiwan's tourist attractions in the realms of culture, nature, food and adventure.

NEXT PAGES –
ADVERTISING
Epic photography shot using a FlyCam represents Taiwan's lesser-known sites, such as the crystalline Sun Moon Lake.

C

Sun Moon Lake, Nantou
The pristine waters of Sun Moon Lake lap at the shores of tiny Lalu Island.

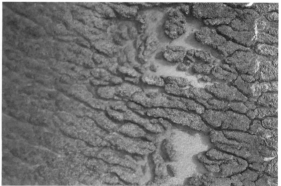

Dive into Taiwan

At first sight of its crystalline lakes and lush gorges, it's abundantly clear why Portuguese explorers called Taiwan 'Formosa', or 'beautiful island'. Two-thirds cloaked by verdant mountains, its eight national parks offer a stunningly diverse landscape to explore, from climbable cliffs and volcanic craters to white coral beaches and tropical forests. On land or on water, it's time to discover one of nature's least-known playgrounds in Taiwan.

Little Liuqiu, Dapeng Bay
This spectacular coral islet boasts azure waters and shell-strewn sandy shores.

The Heart of Nature

THE HEART OF ASIA

www.taiwan.net.tw

Coastal road, Hualien
Emerald cliffs lapped by a glittering sea offer cyclists unforgettable panoramas on Highway 9.

Ready to roll

From exhilarating peaks and lush valleys to perfect lakes, Taiwan offers cyclists some of the world's most spectacular scenery for two-wheeled discovery, all accessible on hundreds of miles of smooth road, protected cycle trails and off-road routes. For relaxed riders or athletic adventurers, there's no better place to explore pristine nature and breathtaking vistas – there are even bike-friendly hotels and restaurants where bikers can pause for refreshment, all while enjoying the nation's famously warm welcome and fabulous food.

Taroko Gorge

Hundreds of feet above water, this gorge crossing is just one of the thrilling moments cycling through Taroko National Park.

The Heart of Cycling

www.taiwan.net.tw

THE HEART OF ASIA

Client
Fukuoka City
Country
Japan
Work
Publishing

Fukuoka is the largest city in Japan's southern Kyushu region and occupies one of the most advantageous positions in Asia. Winkreative was commissioned by the city government to create an informative, multilingual brochure to promote this dynamic metropolis.

Using a reportage-style approach, we explored all aspects of the city, highlighting its buzzing businesses, local craftsmanship, eco-initiatives and connectivity, as well as its strong creative industry. The brochure comes to life with friendly and colourful illustrations and lively photography.

A – BROCHURE
The brochure has a removable illustrated cover.

B – SPREADS
Playful illustrations are mixed with warm and punchy photography, welcoming visitors to the city. A Q&A insert profiles different owners in Fukuoka.

OPPOSITE –
BROCHURE COVER
An illustrated day-to-night scene conveys a 24-hour city.

Charm

Design holds great potential for enjoyment. What we see, read and look at can influence our feelings, moods and sometimes even our behaviour, so at Winkreative we believe that having a little fun should be taken seriously. Let MINI take you on a riotous romp around the globe, glide *Dolce Vita* style through Persol's sun-drenched European adventure, whizz off to the Hamptons in the glossy red glamour of StndAIR's seaplane, learn the pleasurable quirks of TOTO's technology and smile at the swagger of Mr. Porter – the suave, stylish and surprising face of Porter Airlines. Infused with optimism and delightful decorum, communication is key, but a little charm goes a long way.

Back to the Future

Winkreative's collaboration with Porter Airlines started at its launch in 2006, and the partnership continues to bring the "flying refined" philosophy to life. Founder and CEO Robert Deluce tells us about the future of flying.

Robert Deluce has turned the quiet airport of his boyhood into a dynamic urban hub, serving some two million passengers a year. With fast and efficient domestic flights and a transcontinental service in the pipeline, Porter is putting the pleasure back into flying.

Winkreative
It was an interesting time to launch an airline in Canada. What was the impetus behind Porter?

Robert
It started with the concept of an under utilised transportation asset in the form of Billy Bishop Toronto City Airport, where I had learned to fly as a high-school student. It always seemed to me that it was one of the best-located urban airports in the world and wasn't living up to its potential as a catalyst for tourism and economic development, or just generally as a great urban hub. Our feeling was that if we put together a tight concept and an appropriate amount of investment, we'd be able to turn that around. Today, the airport serves some two million-plus passengers per year, up from the 20,000 passengers going through the airport annually before Porter arrived, which points to a certain amount of success for sure.

One of our original goals was to take passengers back to the golden age of travel, when people dressed up for the occasion and were treated with a degree of respect when they got on board an aircraft.

Winkreative
How does the nature of flight in Canada differ from that elsewhere in the world? Would you say there is an agility to it that is unique?

Robert
Canada has a significant geographical mass; in fact, part of its heritage stems from the railway development that linked the country together in the 1800s. Aviation came much later, but it played a significant role, particularly when ensuring that remote communities felt connected to the rest of Canada. We fly to some northern Ontario communities, who rely on air service for access to medical treatment, universities and government and financial resources, so it's vital. If you move further north into the Arctic communities, they couldn't exist without the air services that move people, food and other vital supplies.

Winkreative
How is Porter distinctly Canadian?

Robert
I think there are both tangible and intangible things that set us apart. We've affiliated ourselves with a number of unique and respected Canadian brands. We serve Steam Whistle beer from a small brewery in Toronto and wine from the Jackson-Triggs winery, and the Canadian manufacturer Bombardier makes the actual aircraft. Our brand mascot, Mr. Porter, the illustrated raccoon, represents our home city of Toronto, an urban area with more raccoons per capita than any other city in the world. There's a lot of tangible evidence and other, less obvious things, like the refined nature of our offerings and the high level of service we provide. The Canadian attitude towards these things is very relevant to what we do here at Porter.

Winkreative
How has air travel in Canada changed in the last decade?

Robert
Porter itself has played a role in changing air travel over the past seven years. Our own role in the acceptance and expectation of a premium economy level of service, which isn't an elite service but offers excellent service and value – I think we may well have been among the first to start offering that as an alternative to what was being produced. Our competitors now offer some "Porter perks", which I don't think would exist had we not started offering some of the amenities that are very much associated with Porter today. This premium economy offering is quite separate from the low-cost model that prevailed before we got started, so it's not easyJet or Ryanair. It's something completely different, but at the same time, it's grown to be quite representative of a product that has good value, great service and strong attention to detail. The formula is working because, as air travel has become more convenient and accessible, traffic has risen significantly.

Unfortunately, in terms of security, some travel impediments remain. Despite the constraints, we work hard to turn air travel into a good overall experience. At Billy Bishop, while still maintaining a high level of security and fulfilling all the requirements of a post-9/11 world, we try to turn that experience into something more pleasant and tolerable. We're a lot closer to what travel used to be like a number of years ago when flying was something people looked forward to.

Winkreative
What changes do you see in the next decade?

Robert

We're always at the drawing board, looking at how to refine what we're doing. We hope to grow our own network with a transcontinental service beginning in 2016, which will give our passengers more choice and lead to lower fares, allowing more people to travel. These things continue to evolve, so there's plenty on the horizon.

Winkreative

Do you think it's important for an airline to have a friendly face? How do you balance humanity with efficiency?

Robert

When you have two distinct aspects to your brand, it is a bit of a balancing act. The colour scheme, logo, aircraft livery – all of that gives the impression that Porter is very corporate. On the other hand, there's our illustrated raccoon brand mascot, which allows us to inject fun and playfulness into everything we do, from the advertising and water bottles to the snacks and meal boxes. This helps make our brand approachable while looking businesslike and professional. These unique aspects are pretty evident, and people are quick to recognise and understand what Porter stands for.

Winkreative

What attracted you to Winkreative?

Robert

Ultimately, it was a little bit of its Canadian heritage along with its international outlook. Winkreative has good experience in the transportation sector and had gone through a similar exercise with a European carrier not long before we came knocking, which was important to us. The other thing that has always been a strong point is Tyler's own personal experience as a frequent flyer. Anybody who flies upwards of a couple of hundred days a year has to see and appreciate both the good and the bad of what's out there. That helps when you're trying to do something that's unique and distinct but affordable. The solutions don't have to be grandiose, but they do have to speak of a service that you want people to be attracted to.

Winkreative

What does our aesthetic lend to your business?

Robert

Right from day one we wanted to set ourselves apart from the competition. For a new airline, making sure we established strong brand recognition right from the get-go in a meaningful way was critical. We had limited time to establish our credibility, while our competitors had fairly large war chests, so we needed to do everything we could quickly and well. This required unique thinking. The Porter brand mascot, although controversial at the start, really did end up being an aspect of the brand that helped us to accomplish this. Winkreative has a good reputation with *Wallpaper* and now *Monocle*, and all of that has helped people to access and understand the Porter brand. The other thing we appreciate is Winkreative's focus on the complete experience – it's not just about providing a logo and letterhead and calling it a day. Winkreative extends its attention to pretty much every aspect of the passenger experience. Some of that goes back to the fact that a lot of people in the company travel extensively and understand the difference between what's good and what isn't, and that's essential because the devil is in the detail. Thanks to Winkreative, we've become quite good at putting ourselves out there in a refined way, which gives us an advantage.

For a new airline, making sure we established strong brand recognition right from the get-go in a meaningful way was critical.

Winkreative

Why do you think you are in our "Charm" chapter?

Robert

One of our original goals was to take passengers back to the golden age of travel, when people dressed up for the occasion and were treated with a degree of respect when they got on board an aircraft. In today's world, there's a lot of that missing. For Porter, doing those bits and pieces and putting some of the charm back into flying is beneficial to us, even though we see it as being standard procedure. It's the attention to detail that gives us a certain charm.

Winkreative

What inspires you?

Robert

The airline sector is an unusual business and not for the faint-hearted; that may be an old cliché, but there are always challenges. There's no such thing as putting your feet up or going on autopilot. There are always new challenges, or speed bumps, as we like to call them, but overcoming these challenges is rewarding, and all our team members take great satisfaction from being able to do exactly that. Porter has engendered a lot of goodwill and positive feedback, which is unusual for an airline, and whether you're a pilot a flight attendant or in one of our call centres, that positive feedback is inspiring. So continuing to build on that and improve is our mission, and it's inspiring to see just how far you can take that.

Porter Airlines

Country
Canada
Work
Identity
Publishing
Digital design
Advertising
Environment
Animation

Porter is a Toronto-based airline geared to savvy weekend and business travellers. It is marketed as an efficient and innovative alternative to traditional airlines serving the US and Canadian markets for passengers on short-haul routes. Involved from the start, Winkreative has developed a comprehensive corporate identity for Porter, including name, logotype, colour palette, livery design, printed materials and website.

Following a successful launch, the scope of the project has included the design of cabin interiors and uniforms, an in-flight magazine, passenger items, advertising and an illustrated raccoon mascot. This relationship has helped Porter restore the sense of dignity and refinement once associated with flying.

A – NAME
The naming of Porter was a significant part of the branding. The name works in both French and English and has the desired connotations of transporting with care.

B – LOGO
The airline's mascot is the raccoon, Mr. Porter, a savvy creature and a national icon.

A

porter

B

re:porter

The journal of Porter Airlines
Le journal des lignes aériennes Porter

25
Nov/Dec
Nov/Déc
2012

Weekender
Mush ado – the pulling power of Mont Tremblant
Le pouvoir d'attraction de Mont-Tremblant

PREVIOUS PAGES –
LIVERY
Winkreative designed the livery and oversaw the entire application process.

A – *RE:PORTER* COVER
Huskies were photographed for a Christmas issue of Porter's in-flight magazine, *re:porter,* to promote the area of Mont Tremblant. The measurements of the magazine were designed specifically to ensure the title appears above the top of the seat pocket.

B

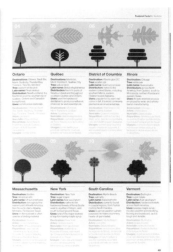

C

Petoskey is a compact place, great for walking around downtown, and even better or bicycling into nature. Its downtown is just a few streets wide by a few streets long, but is so packed with intriguing stores and eateries, you can spend days exploring here.

Closer to the lake, you'll find a summer-long rotation of events and festivals – the high season starts in July – and live musicians perform at the city park three days a week. It's also where you'll find the Little Traverse History Museum, which

specializes in Hemingway's connection with Petoskey. The writer spent the summers of his youth and beyond in the area, from 1899 to 1921, and he later used it as a setting for short stories and his first novella, *The Torrents of Spring*. His ghost is still very much in evidence: the city is dotted with plaques pointing out buildings that influenced the writer's life and appeared in his fiction.

There's a more direct connection, too: under the enormous leaded mirrors of the City Park Grill, Hemingway's portrait hangs behind the bar,

D

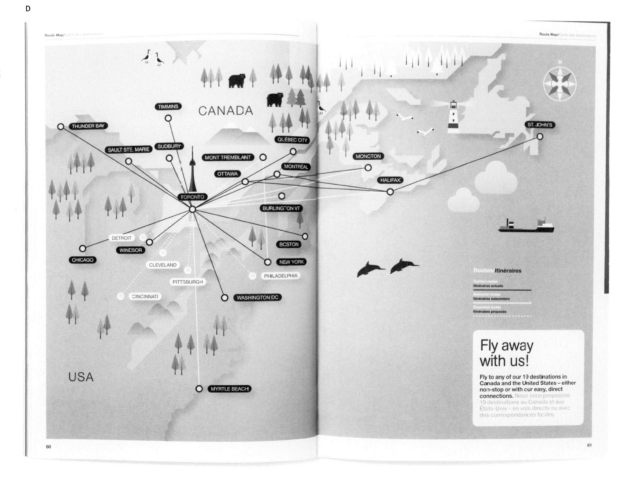

B, C – SPREADS
Features combine lifestyle photography with illustration and comprehensive city and neighbourhood guides.

D – MAP
A simple illustrated map shows Porter's destinations.

Keep an eye out.

Keep an eye out.

porter

flying refined

www.flyporter.com

A

Keep an eye out.

porter
flying refined

www.flyporter.com

B

Here comes the pitch…

porter

It's a grand slam of a sale – enjoy huge savings on all Porter flights.

Summer is here, and to celebrate the sunniest season, Porter is offering mercury-popping savings on all base fares. Plus, our comfortable Toronto lounge and friendly in-flight service means all our passengers feel like all-stars. Act fast to take advantage of this huge sale: It's one you won't want to miss.

Flights from Toronto: Book by March 23. Book online, call 1-888-619-8622 or contact your travel agent.

HALIFAX 6 x daily	MONCTON 4 x weekly	MONT TREMBLANT 12 x weekly	MONTRÉAL 20 x daily	OTTAWA 21 x daily	QUÉBEC CITY 3 x daily	ST. JOHN'S 3 x daily	SAULT STE. MARIE 2 x daily starting May 4
$149*	$159*	$79*	$149*	$139*	$119*	$169*	$99*
SUDBURY Daily	THUNDER BAY 3 x daily	WINDSOR 3 x daily starting April 27	BOSTON 6 x daily	CHICAGO 6 x daily	MYRTLE BEACH 4 x weekly	NEW YORK 11 x daily	TIMMINS 2 x weekly
$109*	$149*	$79*	$149*	$139*	$179*	$149*	$149*
BURLINGTON, VT 3 x weekly	WASHINGTON COMING SOON						
$109*	$149*						

Book by March 23, 2011. Travel by June 23, 2011. Travel by April 5, 2011 for Mont Tremblant, and travel by May 23, 2011 for Myrtle Beach. Some fares may require up to 21 day advance purchase. Fares are one-way in Firm class and do not include taxes, fees or surcharges. A return trip is not required to qualify for this one-way fare. Seats at these fares are limited and may not be available on all flights. New bookings only.

flyporter.com

PREVIOUS PAGE, A –
PRE-LAUNCH TEASER
Porter is coming...

B,C – ADVERTISING
Winkreative produces
an ongoing series of ads
for promotions, sales and
company news.

Got long legs?
You'll love Porter.

You already know that Porter isn't like other airlines. Here's one
of many reasons why: Our seats, which are real leather, offer
more leg room than any of our competitors' economy seats on
the routes we fly. So if you are long of limb, you can be sure that
Porter will offer comfort unlike any other.

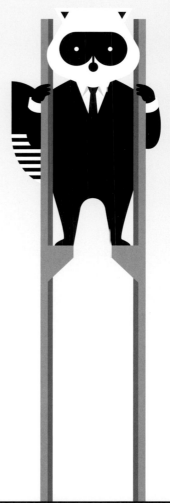

Flights from Toronto: Book by March 23. Book online, call 1-888-619-8622 or contact your travel agent.

HALIFAX 6 x daily	MONCTON 4 x weekly	MONT TREMBLANT 12 x weekly	MONTRÉAL 20 x daily	OTTAWA 21 x daily	QUÉBEC CITY 3 x daily	ST. JOHN'S 3 x daily	SAULT STE. MARIE 2 x daily starting May 4
$149*	$159*	$79*	$149*	$139*	$119*	$169*	$99*

SUDBURY Daily	THUNDER BAY 3 x daily	WINDSOR 3 x daily starting April 27	BOSTON 5 x daily	CHICAGO 6 x daily	MYRTLE BEACH 4 x weekly	NEW YORK 11 x daily	TIMMINS 2 x weekly
$109*	$149*	$79*	$149*	$139*	$179*	$149*	$149*

BURLINGTON, VT 3 x weekly	WASHINGTON COMING SOON
$109*	$149*

Book by March 23, 2011. Travel by June 23, 2011. Travel by April 3, 2011 for Mont Tremblant, and travel by
May 23, 2011 for Myrtle Beach. Some fares may require up to 21 day advance purchase. Fares are one-way
in Firm class and do not include taxes, fees or surcharges. A return trip is not required to qualify for this
one-way fare. Seats at these fares are limited and may not be available on all flights. New bookings only.

flyporter.com

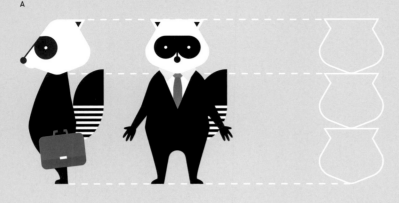

A – MR. PORTER
A selection of the many guises, poses and skills of this multi-talented mascot.

NEXT PAGE – ANIMATION
Mr. Porter was brought to life for a series of animated TV ads.

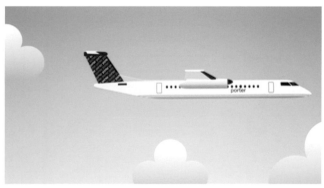

The Path to Enlightenment

In the East, the bathroom is a place for achieving physical and spiritual well-being, where time spent can be the relaxing, meditative core of each day. As Japanese food and design continue to influence the lifestyle of Europeans, TOTO believes that Japan's traditional bathroom culture is next.

In his 1933 essay on aesthetics, the Japanese author Junichirō Tanizaki said: "Anyone with a taste for traditional architecture must agree that the Japanese toilet is perfection." Historically, the toilet was a closed, personal space set apart from the main house and often "made from finely grained wood in a grove fragrant with leaves". These tranquil surroundings enshrined the toilet as a pleasant place to listen to birdsong or the chirping of insects, watch the moon or simply spend time achieving "true spiritual repose".

The same cannot be said of Western water closets. Historically, the toilet has been regarded as utterly unclean, and any mention of it in polite conversation is avoided at all costs. However, the Japanese sanitary company TOTO is changing that perception. With TOTO encouraging Europeans to follow in the enlightened footsteps of the Japanese, could a trip to a European toilet become an opportunity to improve physical and spiritual well-being?

Kazuchika Okura founded TOTO in 1917. After five years of experimenting in his ceramics laboratory, he finally mastered the art of making ceramic toilet bowls, which were common in Europe and America. Today, TOTO embodies four key areas of Japanese culture that show the way forward – technology, design, luxury and well-being. Of all its perfectly crafted and technologically expert bathroom and kitchen products, the Washlet is TOTO's signature design, with sales of more than 34 million since its invention in 1980.

Almost ubiquitous in Japan (70 per cent of Japanese households have one), the Washlet combines the core Japanese values of innovative technology and good design, creating a toilet with relaxing and restorative elements inspired by traditional Japanese bathroom culture. This small, free-standing unit has an adjustable heated seat (the comfort of a warm seat on a cold day cannot be underestimated), the ability to both wash and dry its user, antibacterial water to break down waste, a non-stick hygienic glaze (fairly self-explanatory) and a revolutionary tornado flush system that tackles even the most dangerous of deposits while still saving water.

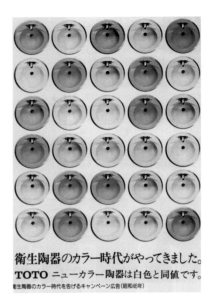

衛生陶器のカラー時代がやってきました。
TOTO ニューカラー陶器は白色と同値です。
衛生陶器のカラー時代を告げるキャンペーン広告(昭和46年)

The special features of its more exclusive models show a typically Japanese, technology-obsessed mind at work, where every detail of both the product and the atmosphere it creates is considered. The bathroom door, toilet seat and flush are all sensor-activated, so users never actually touch anything with their hands. TOTO has developed a Washlet with small LED lights that illuminate in the dark. Never again do users have to suffer the blinding beam of the bathroom light in the middle of the night: instead the Washlet casts a gentle glow onto the walls around it, which guides them through the darkness to the warm ceramic throne.

Warmth, cleanliness and mood lighting – Junichirō Tanizaki's three prerequisites for the perfect toilet create a place not only for use but also for enjoyment. Add some music and light reading to the mix (some of the newer models are kitted out with shelves and MP3 players), and the toilet once again becomes a sphere of well-being.

TOTO has been developed to create harmony between body and mind through the perfect bathroom experience. While many of the merits of Japanese culture, such as the beneficial and aesthetic nature of its food, the purity of its design and the peace and repose of its traditional living, already strongly influence the lifestyle of Europeans, perhaps TOTO will help contribute yet another.

新発売
NEW TOTO 鋳鉄ホーローバス TOTO 東陶

PREVIOUS PAGE
The TOTO family in 1917; toilet production in 1923.

ABOVE AND LEFT
TOTO advertising from 1980; TOTO advertising from 1981.

TOTO

Country
Japan

Work
**Strategy
Identity
Publishing
Digital design
Advertising
Environment
Animation**

Winkreative developed the complete strategy, concept and creative direction for the European launch of Japan's leading toilet and sanitaryware company, TOTO, in 2009. Since then, Winkreative has been pivotal in anchoring the creative expression of the TOTO brand on the benefits of Japanese culture related to technology, well-being, luxury and design.

For the 2013 edition of the International Sanitary and Heating (ISH) trade show in Frankfurt, Winkreative crafted TOTO's exhibition concepts, from signage to brochures and advertisements, and oversaw the art direction of promotional movies and a video animation. Additionally, Winkreative commissioned MACH Architektur to design concepts for showrooms and exhibitions at ISH, as well as at the Salone Internazionale del Mobile in Milan.

A – PRODUCT LAUNCH CATALOGUE
TOTO launched in Europe with a focus on its premium, technologically innovative product lines to position itself distinctively in the market.

A

A – ICONS
TOTO's technologies were new to the European market, so a language that would educate without being too dry was needed. Each icon is illustrated and explained in the catalogue, making it easier to understand the complexity of the technology. The black icons denote function, and the grey icons allude to benefits, such as those related to the environment and water-saving.

B – PRODUCT CATALOGUES
Each white product catalogue is assigned a bright colour to identify the different product ranges.

B

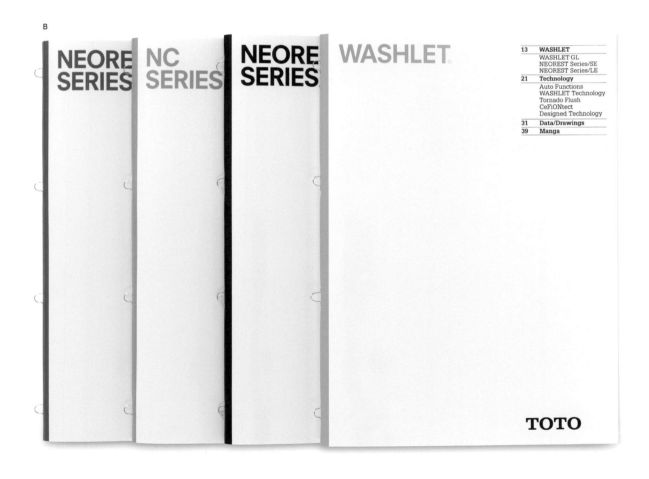

TOTO

C

C – CATALOGUE SPREAD
A Japanese sense of purity prevails with the use of Japanese materials in lifestyle and still-life photography.

D – TECHNOLOGY
Not shy in presenting the toilet as a hero, each technology zone is featured on a black page, with clearly contrasting white identifiers.

NEXT PAGES –
ILLUSTRATION
The different TOTO toilet ranges are celebrated with various forms of illustration, including manga for the Washlet model.

D

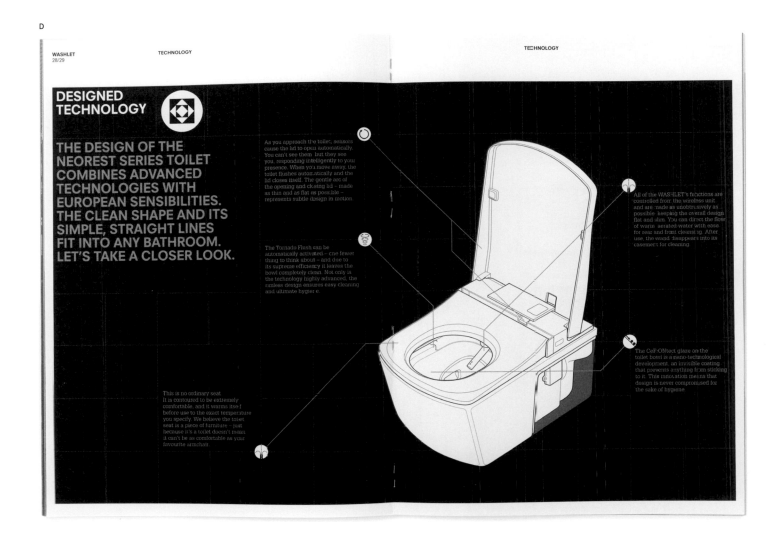

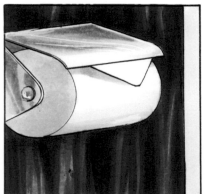

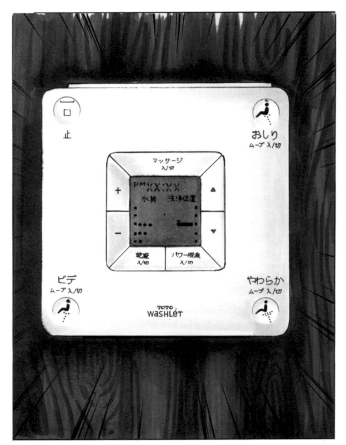

WHAT IS THAT?!

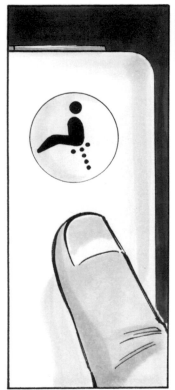

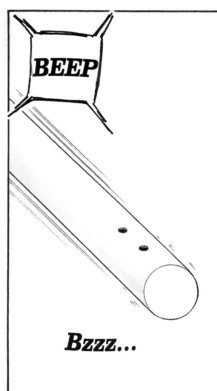

WHOA!

WHAT ON EARTH...?! WAS THAT SPRAY? THAT WAS AN INTERESTING SURPRISE!

BEEP BEEP BEEP

PM

水勢

乾燥
入/切

マッサージ
入/切

DRY ON/OFF   STRENGTH   MASSAGE ON/OFF

SO MANY BUTTONS AND BEEPS! HOW THE HELL DO YOU TURN THIS THING OFF?

WHAT A WONDERFULLY REFRESHING EXPERIENCE...

NOW THIS HAS TO BE RIPE FOR GLOBAL EXPORT...

A – ANIMATION
Launch animation by Kuntzel + Deygas.

B – MARKETING BROCHURE
The marketing brochure has a screen-printed cover and includes typographic statements to guide the reader through the milestones of TOTO's history.

C, NEXT PAGES – ADVERTISING
The ad campaigns contain lifestyle imagery, over-printed with the technology icons to explain the benefits of each product.

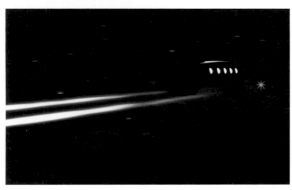

B

CLEAN TECHNOLOGY SINCE 1917
WHAT IT DOES HOW IT FEELS HOW IT WORKS WHERE IT'S FROM WHEN IT STARTED WHY YOU NEED IT TODAY AND EVERYDAY

TOTO

02/03

OUR LAUNCH IN EUROPE IS THE NATURAL NEXT STEP. WE WANT EVERYONE TO KNOW THAT OUR PRODUCTS CAN HAVE WONDERFUL BENEFITS FOR LIFESTYLE, CLEANLINESS AND ECOLOGY.

Clean Technology is the phrase that best sums up what TOTO is about. It is a principle that has guided the company since its founding, and is a completely new concept for the European bathroom. This is how we define it in five simple points.

WHAT IS CLEAN TECHNOLOGY?

1
The future of the bathroom

Just as technology has revolutionised every aspect of contemporary life, TOTO's innovations are changing the way people think about and use bathrooms. TOTO embrace technology in the pursuit of cleanliness, the same way it is embraced in the workplace for efficiency, or in social environments for communication and leisure.

2
The key to a better lifestyle

TOTO's products allow for previously unimaginable levels of cleanliness, relaxation and contentment. Cleaning with warm water is not only hygienic, it is enjoyable and comfortable for everyone from children to seniors. Clean Technology is all about making time spent in the bathroom more fulfilling.

3
A design philosophy

TOTO discreetly incorporates Clean Technology into its products with a sophisticated eye for design. This results in high aesthetic standards for both individual items that blend unobtrusively into their surroundings, and for perfectly coordinated suites. But the TOTO design philosophy goes beyond aesthetics: every product facilitates easy, comfortable usage for every potential user, from children to the elderly, providing Clean Technology for everyone.

4
Environmental benefits

For technology to be truly clean it must do more than enhance personal cleanliness – it must also lead to a cleaner, greener environment. Every time you use a TOTO bathroom, our general mantra of saving energy and water wherever possible, other eco-friendly effects are achieved with our products – our custom ceramic surfaces require fewer chemicals for cleaning; one of our technologies breaks down pollutants in the air, similar to the way a tree breaks down carbon; and some of our fixtures are powered by water pressure alone. All of these features are sustainable.

5
A guiding principle

Since its founding in 1917, TOTO has worked towards an ideal of cleanliness and comfort, with technology becoming ever more integral in achieving it. As TOTO launches in Europe, bringing the potential for an enhanced lifestyle, more beautiful bathrooms and a healthier planet, the philosophy of Clean Technology will remain the company's guiding principle.

C

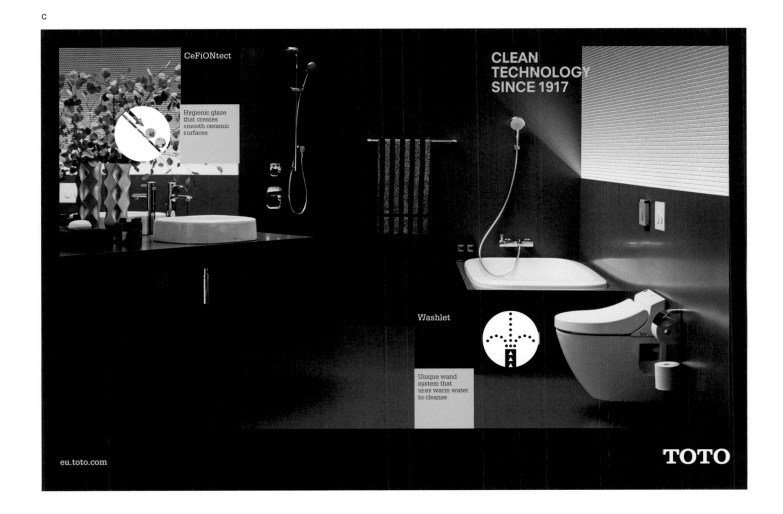

Luminist

Transluscent epoxy resin material

Gyrostream

Tilting and rotating shower water nozzles

CLEAN
TECHNOLOGY
SINCE 1917

Auto
Functions

Technologies
activated
by human
movement

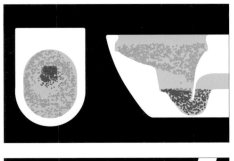
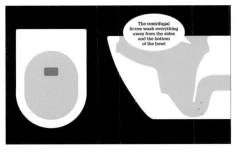
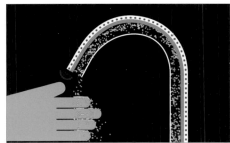

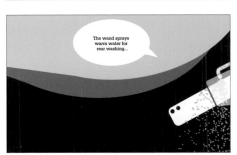
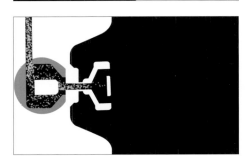
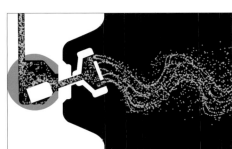
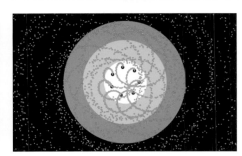

A – EXHIBITION SPACE
Inspired by traditional Japanese design and interpreted through a modern lens, the form, materials and content display were specified to create the clean and open TOTO space at the ISH trade show.

B – WEBSITE
The website features a series of animations, a design collaboration with Universal Everything.

C – EXHIBITION BROCHURE
Based on a lifestyle approach, the concept for the ISH exhibition brochure revolves around the perfect day.

NEXT PAGES – ILLUSTRATION
ISH exhibition brochure illustrations.

C

PERFECT BATHROOM. PERFECT DAY.

TOTO

7am
WAKE-UP TIME
—

**A GENTLY MASSAGING
SHOWER GETS THE DAY
OFF TO A PERFECT START**

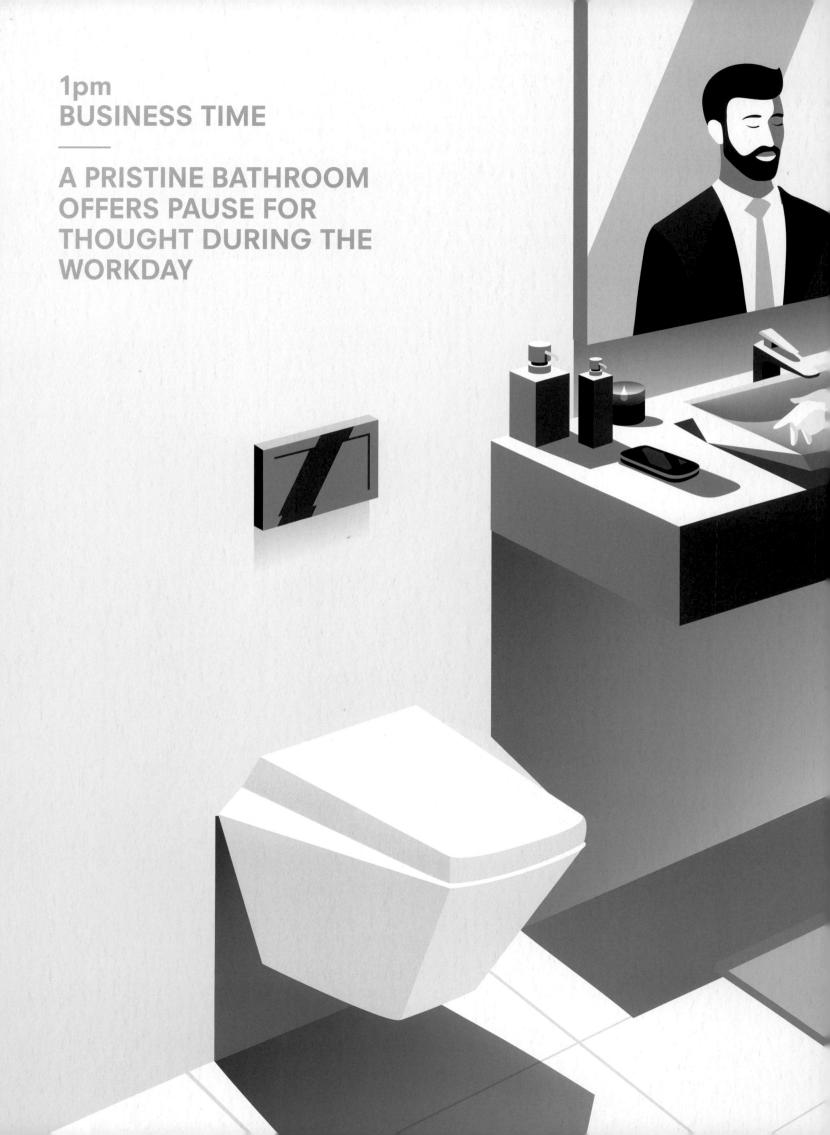

1pm
BUSINESS TIME

A PRISTINE BATHROOM OFFERS PAUSE FOR THOUGHT DURING THE WORKDAY

7.30pm
CALM-DOWN TIME
—
NOTHING RELAXES
LIKE A SUMPTUOUS
SOAK AFTER THE DAY'S
WORK IS DONE

ADVERTISING FILM
Continuing the "perfect day" theme, the film starts with sunrise in a serene Japanese house. Using sensual lighting techniques and a Japanese aesthetic, the film reveals all the functions of this new model, with none of the glare of traditional bathroom advertising.

NEOREST

Charm can be brought to life in many ways. Bulldogs, raccoons and roosters, bold colours and sunny skies – these are just a few of the ways we like to have fun.

Projects
Persol | Francfranc
MINI | Mori Building
Taoyuan International Airport
Cornèr Bank | StndAIR

Client
Persol

Country
Italy

Work
**Packaging
Animation**

Take one globetrotting character, a series of sun-drenched adventures and a stylish suite of accessories, and you have the basic ingredients for *A Year of Sun* – the Winkreative-produced film for luxury eyewear brand Persol.

Assembling a hugely talented team of contributors, Winkreative devised a character and story line to bring the brand's iconic "between you and the sun" strapline to life. Tracking

an urbane gentleman as he roams the world in an endless, retro-styled summer, the animation was the product of intense collaboration and was greeted by popular and critical acclaim.

Winkreative also conceived the idea of a limited-edition box for Persol's classic sunglasses. Crafted in Japan from walnut wood and lined with velvety suede, the case is every bit as covetable as the glasses inside.

A, OPPOSITE –
ANIMATION
Capturing the Persol lifestyle, the animation follows this stylish gent on a European jaunt of sun, leisure, culture - and sunglasses. Animation © Luxottica Group S.p.A

A

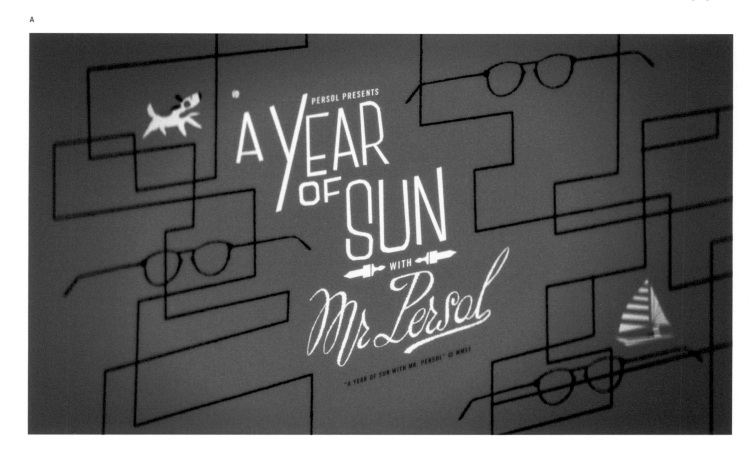

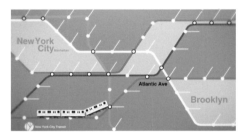

Persol Charm

A – PACKAGING
The Japanese-crafted
walnut wood collectors'
boxes. Packaging ©
Luxottica Group S.p.A

A

Client
Francfranc

Country
Japan

Work
**Identity
Publishing
Digital design
Advertising**

Francfranc is an iconic Japanese interiors retailer with stores in Japan, Hong Kong and Korea. To differentiate Francfranc in the competitive Japanese lifestyle market, Winkreative redesigned the existing identity and performed a positioning exercise that resulted in the production of a brand book to enable Francfranc to effectively communicate its vision to expanding markets.

In addition to the book, Winkreative crafted a new marque, equally suited to signage and products.

We also devised an advertising campaign for the brand's flagship store in Tokyo, depicting Francfranc's role at the heart of the Japanese high street, and created an iPad app to engage with customers and bring the collection to life.

Championing the range of quality lifestyle products, the app features short stop-motion films depicting the fun personalities of the teacups, pillows, clocks and dispenser bottles, with the option of perusing the individual products in generous close-up. A colourful tribute ensues.

A

Living redefined
新しい日常へ

A – MARQUE
Incorporating the existing Helvetica font, we refreshed the logo into a button-style stamp.

B – BRAND BOOK
This internal publication was the new vision for the brand.

NEXT PAGES – POSTER
The brochure's linen-bound cover has a wraparound poster that folds out into the perfect high street.

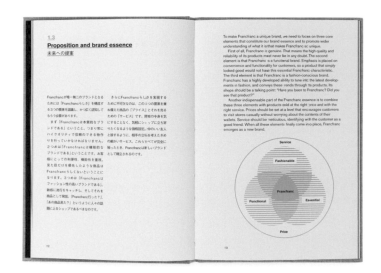

Work
ワーク

Cook
クッキング

Client
MINI

Country
Germany

Work
**Publishing
Digital design**

To set MINI apart from other automotive brands, Winkreative relaunched its global consumer magazine, *The MINI International,* with a full editorial and design overhaul. To capture MINI's sense of irreverent adventure, the magazine boasts a lively design and layout, playful typography, vibrant photography and quirky characters, as well as compelling editorial

content. A collectible title for the curious minded, *The MINI International* takes readers on a riotous romp around the globe, with editions available in eight languages.

A complementary iPad app adds an interactive dimension to the print edition, with its intuitive navigation, exclusive iPad-only films and shareable content.

A

A,C – MAGAZINE
The MINI International draws together disparate elements of contemporary culture to inform creativity around MINI vehicles.

B – ILLUSTRATION
Miles and Spike accompany the reader on the journey through the magazine.

D – CONTENTS PAGE
Elements such as the road marking-inspired graphic symbols are used to convey speed and dynamism in the magazine.

B

CONTENTS

CHUGGA-BOOM

39

9 CONTRIBUTORS
WHO WE ARE
Illustration, photography, whatever the medium, we meet the talents behind Issue 39.

11 THE DASH
33 THINGS WE LOVE
This summer we're loving leather footballs, skateboards, swimming trunks and colourful camping cups.

21 THE DRIVE
MY MINI JOURNEY
Designer Rasmus Ibfelt puts the cool back in Copenhagen on a tour of his hometown.

24 EXTRA MILER
MARSEILLE MISTRAL
Local skateboarder Alex Attali is no stranger to speed and adrenaline, and now – in the MINI John Cooper Works Paceman – he's setting his heart racing on the road, too.

36 MODORAMA
FAMILY AFFAIR
A look at the fantastic MINI family that is John Cooper Works, plus a spotlight on the MINI Clubman Bond Street and the brand new MINI Paceman.

44 DRIVE-BY
THRILLING STATION
An up-close look at Viamala Raststätte Thusis, Switzerland.

46 MINI MASTER
SOUNDS GOOD
An interview with Jacopo Marchetti, a MINI noise, vibration and harshness engineer, and a behind-the-scenes peek at his workplace.

50 NAVIGATOR
10 YEARS IN CASABLANCA
On a drive through Casablanca in the MINI Clubman Bond Street, with travel writer Tahir Shah and his wife, Rachana, we discover why the pair left London a decade ago for this colourful city on the Moroccan coast.

60 CREATIVE USE OF SPACE
WHANGAPOUA SLED HOUSE
One minute it's there, the next it's gone. Welcome to the Whangapoua Sled House, a removable holiday home in New Zealand.

64 MINI-ME
WALK OF LIFE
We meet four owners who love their MINIs, from countries across the globe.

66 SERIAL NUMBER
DESIGN YOUR OWN CAR
For this competition, we called on the worldwide MINI community to get creative and design their own MINI Clubvans.

68 MINI REPORT
SNEAKER CRAZY / MOD 'N' MINI NIGHT
We meet MINI driver and sneaker enthusiast Wali Wasiri, and take a drive to London's Ace Cafe for its monthly Mod 'n' Mini night.

Technical data is correct at the time of going to press and is subject to change.

Car models shown may not be available in all countries. Please contact your local MINI dealer for more information.

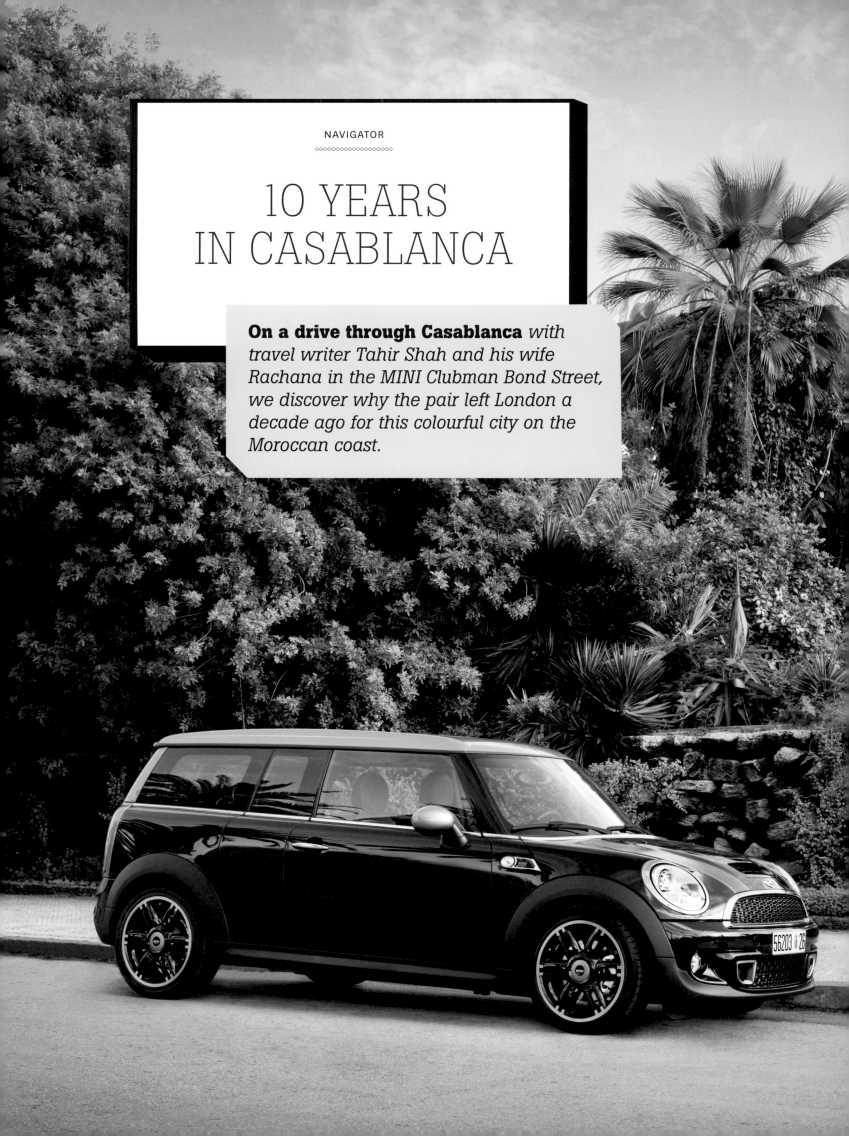

10 YEARS IN CASABLANCA

On a drive through Casablanca *with travel writer Tahir Shah and his wife Rachana in the MINI Clubman Bond Street, we discover why the pair left London a decade ago for this colourful city on the Moroccan coast.*

B

A

PREVIOUS PAGES –
SPREAD
New MINI models are
featured within the main
editorial articles.

A – GRAPHIC ELEMENT
The colour and style of
The Dash graphic are
based on the iconic MINI
dashboard.

C – ILLUSTRATION
Characterful illustration
highlights key aspects of
the features.

C

D

B,D – SPREADS
Going off-grid creates movement on the inside spreads.

E – SPREADS
"The Drive" is a photo-driven piece using personal photographs, offering a glimpse into an international city through the eyes of a MINI driver.

NEXT PAGES –
PHOTOGRAPHY

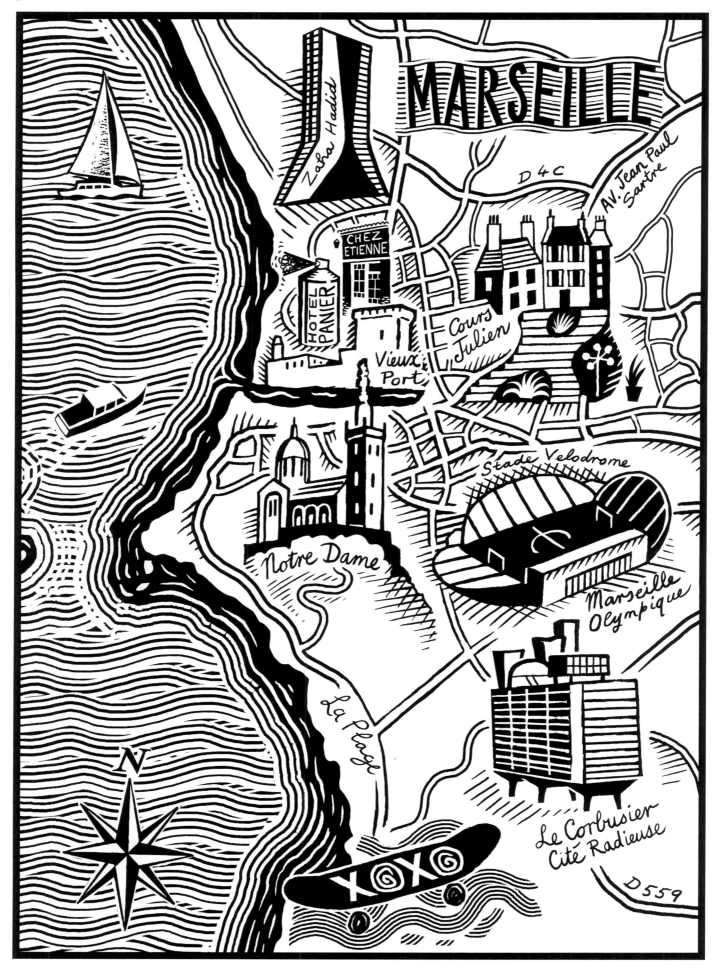

B – IPAD APP
The iPad app transforms
the magazine into
an interactive user
experience and includes
two exclusive iPad-only
films per issue.

B

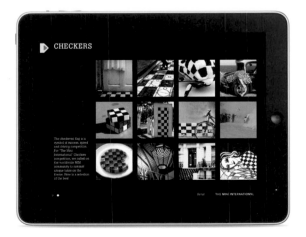

Client
Mori Building
Country
Japan
Work
Publishing

Toranomon Hills is a significant mixed-use development in the Toranomon district of Tokyo that will open in 2014 as one of the city's tallest buildings. The 52-storey tower will include offices, a conference centre, apartments, premium shops and Japan's first Andaz hotel. Like Mori Building's other projects, Roppongi Hills and Omotesando Hills, this large-scale project is set to transform the area around it – pushing traffic underground, creating leafy, bicycle-friendly boulevards and reinvigorating green spaces where families, residents, visitors and workers can enjoy the new neighbourhood. It is part of a joint venture with the Tokyo Metropolitan Government.

ToMoTo Times is a 16-page dual-language newspaper edited and designed by Winkreative to mark the development project. Acting as both a PR/sales tool and an informative guide, *ToMoTo Times* uses the form of a neighbourhood rag and includes interviews with local residents and workers, historians familiar with the area and the architects who designed the tower.

With on-the-ground reporting and charming illustrations, the publication serves as a friendly introduction to one of Tokyo's most important recent urban-regeneration projects.

A – FRONT AND BACK COVERS
Illustrated front and back covers introduce the concept of Toranomon Hills.

A

PREVIOUS PAGE, NEXT
PAGE – PHOTOGRAPHY
Winkreative art-directed
photography to bring the
neighbourhood to life.

A,B – ILLUSTRATION
A map of the
development's
surrounding area shows
all aspects of life at
Toranomon Hills,
from its community
to its proximity to
Tokyo's business district.

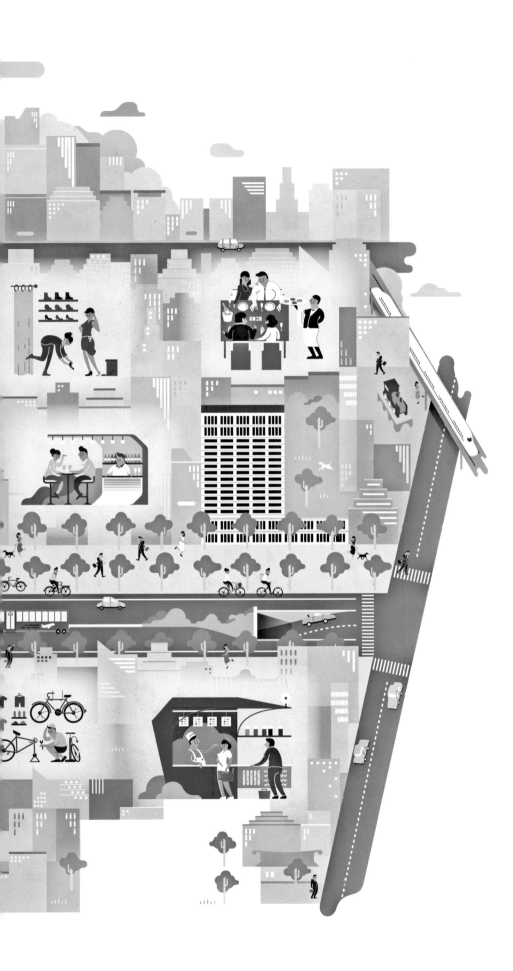

B

Client
Taoyuan International Airport

Country
Taiwan

Work
Strategy
Publishing

Following several information gathering trips to the site of Taoyuan International Airport, Winkreative drafted a strategy for its expansion. By studying the airport's demographics, surrounding areas and existing plans, we translated the client's vision into a clear strategic narrative in the form of a comprehensive book.

With illustration, copywriting and art direction by Winkreative, the book is a lively, accessible and straightforward representation of the concept for Taoyuan International Airport.

A – SPREADS
Based on the perfect journey, the book is a guide to the high-quality services and facilities that Taoyuan will provide.

B, NEXT PAGES – COVER
The cover doubles as a poster that can be removed and unfolded to reveal the full impact of the Taoyuan vision.

A

B

Client
Cornèr Bank
Country
Switzerland
Work
Identity

Winkreative designed a number of credit cards for Cornèr Bank's 18- to 35-year-old target market. Collaborating with the Melbourne-based design and art group Rinzen, Winkreative developed distinctive animal characters. This modern, playful direction was devised to bring

wit and personality to a traditionally sober area of graphic design. At the same time, a sophisticated colour palette was applied to ensure that the bank's reputation for reliability and trust was communicated.

A

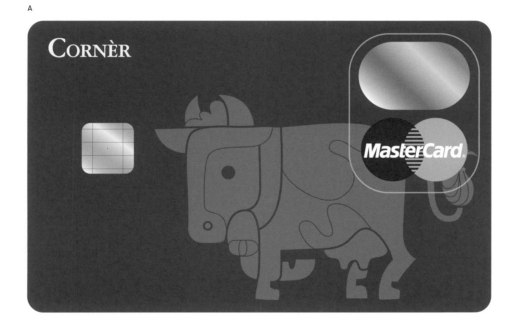

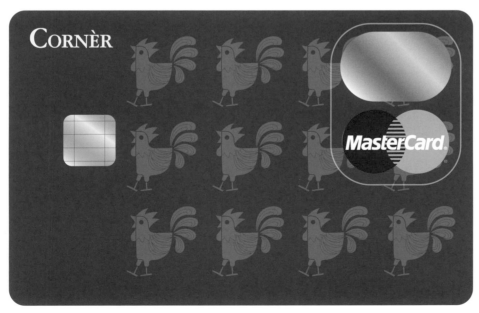

A – CARD ILLUSTRATIONS
The illustrated characters are rooted in classic Swiss mid-century children's books.

Client
StndAIR

Country
United States

Work
Identity
Digital design

A – SEAPLANE
The exterior attracts
attention, noticeable
even from afar.

B, C – IDENTITY
Bold and directional,
the marque and logo
reflect the spirit of
The Standard.

Winkreative believes that there's always room for a little attention-seeking. An innovation from The Standard Hotels, StndAIR is a customised seaplane offering lucky travellers an enviable transfer between Manhattan and Sunset Beach on Shelter Island and the Hamptons. Winkreative and The Standard's in-house design team collaboratively devised a glossy, red and unashamedly bold exterior featuring a bespoke S device capturing the speed of flight. Inspired by sun-kissed skin, in rich, warm colours and luxe finishes, the interiors are inviting but modest enough for passengers to step on board with sandy, bare feet. Winkreative was later commissioned to design a website.

A

Shape-shifters

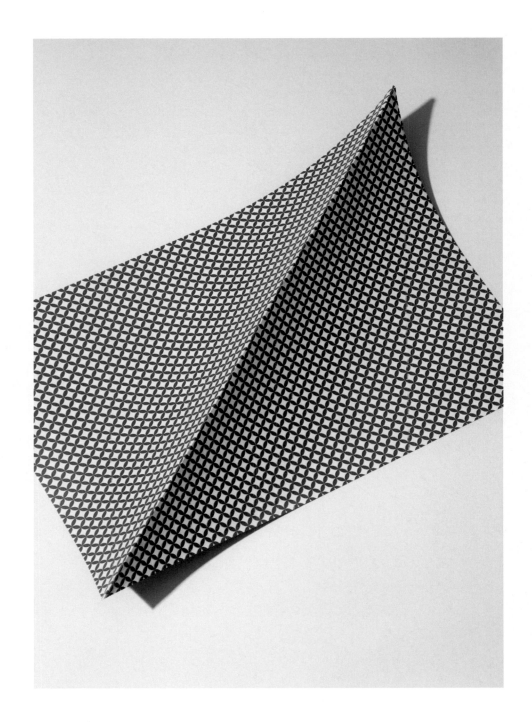

Photography by Matthieu Lavanchy
Styling by Sam Logan

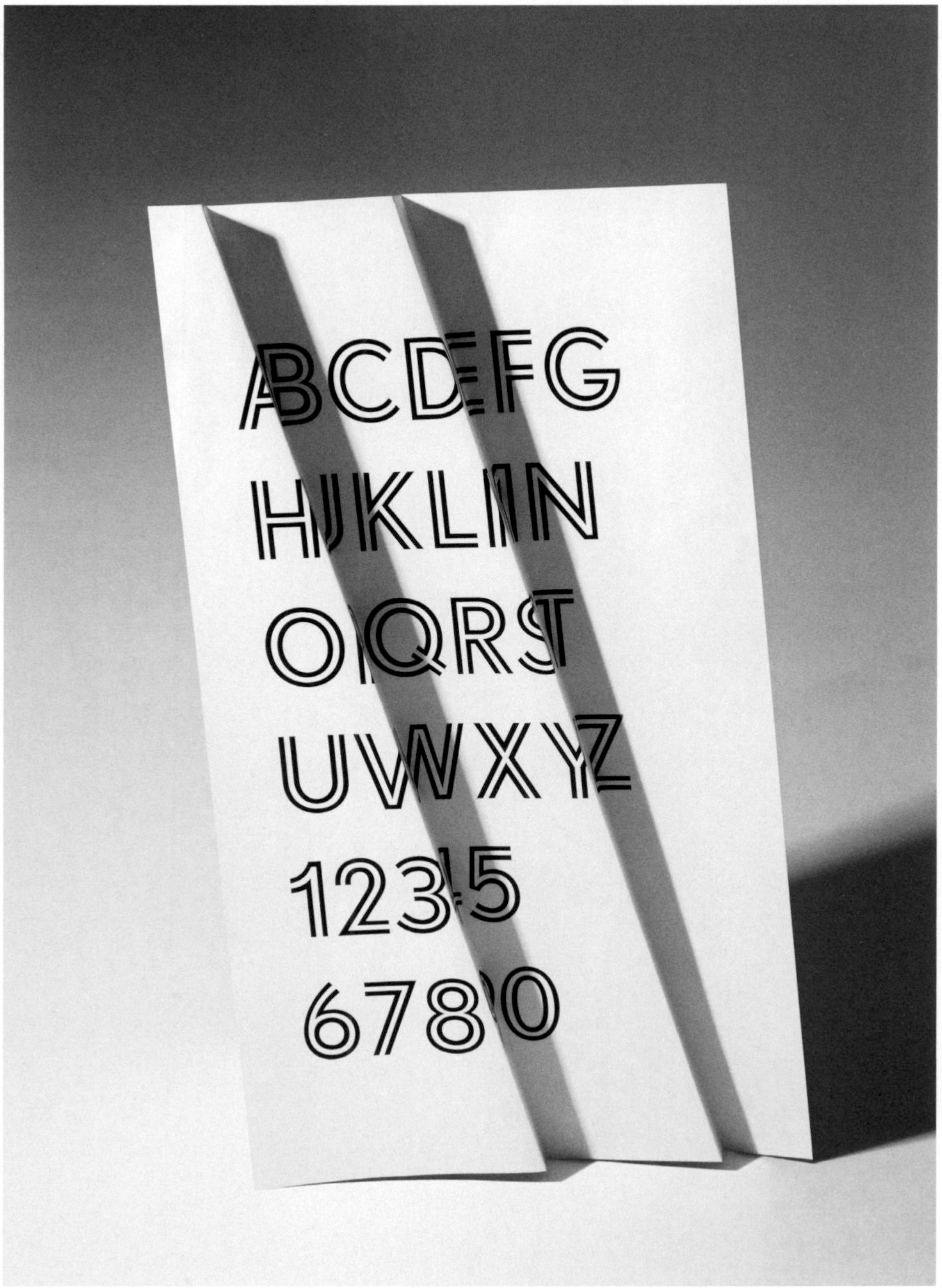

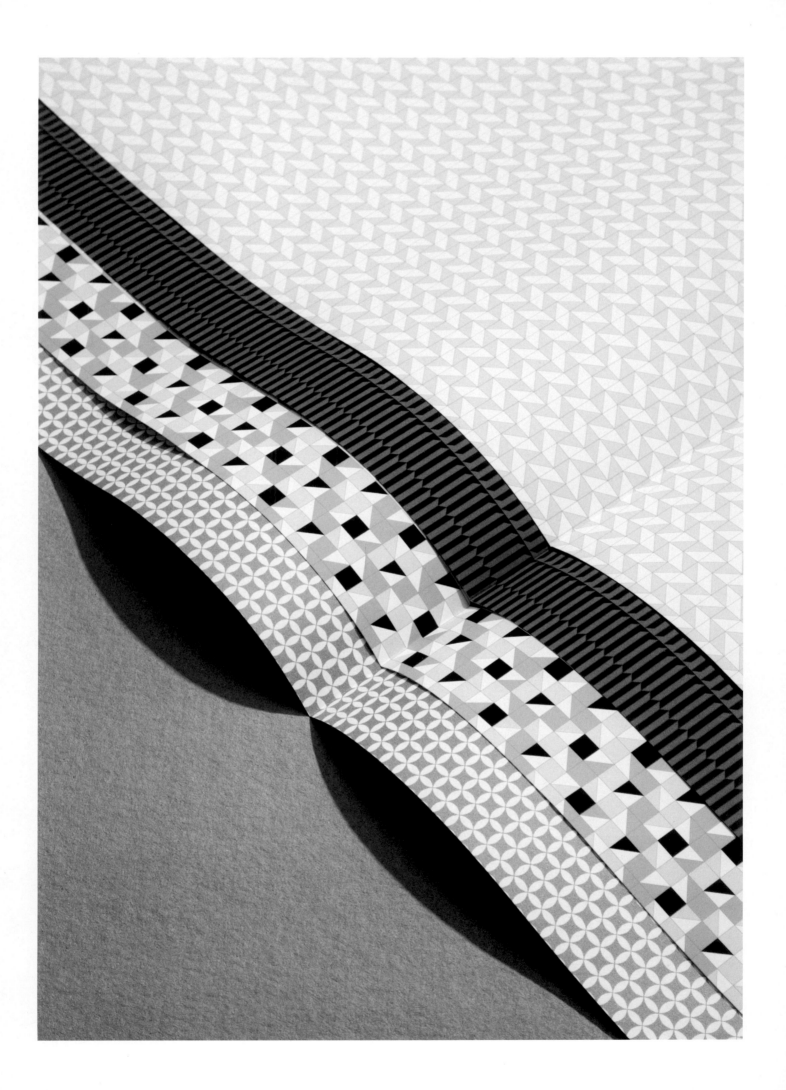

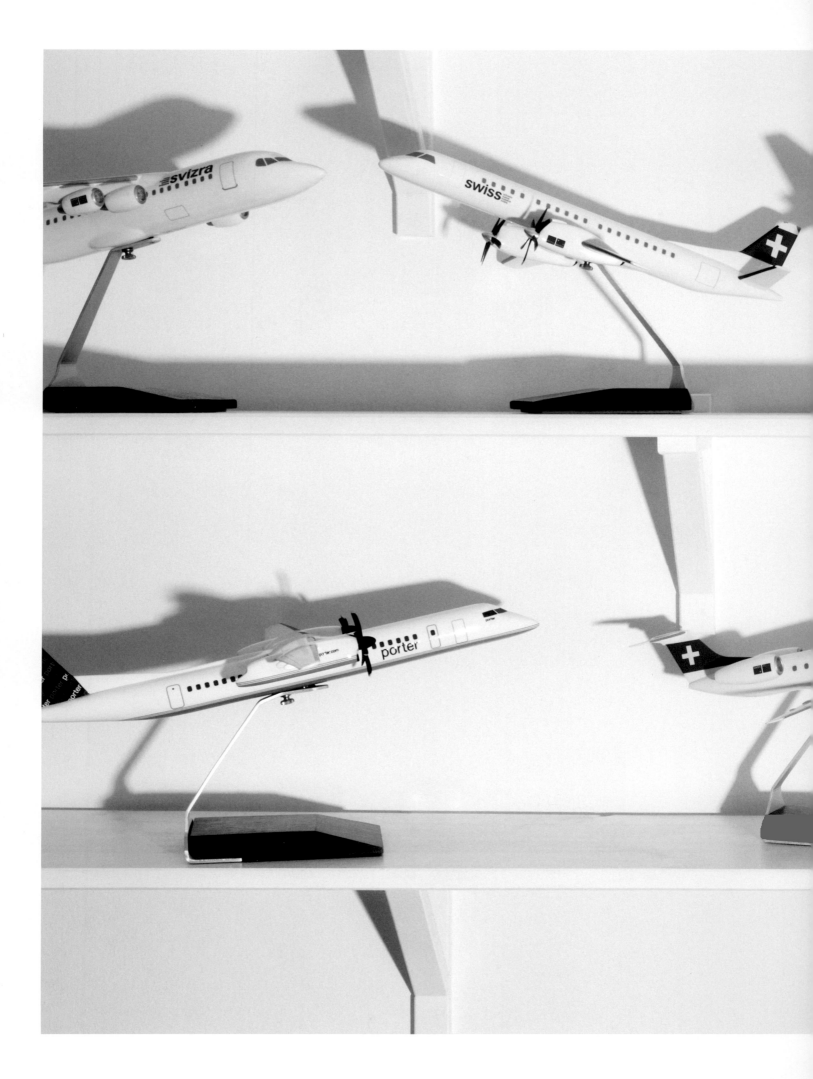

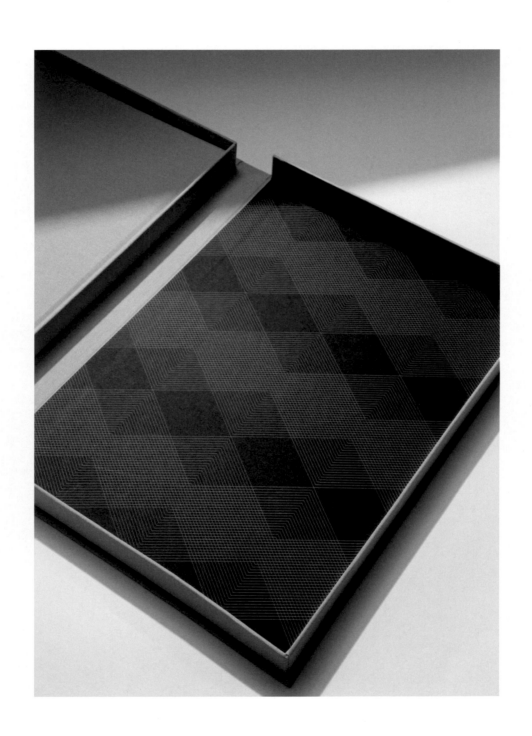

Intelligence

The word "design" can sound cosmetic; indeed, much of what we do is based on aesthetics. But everybody knows that looking good isn't enough – good design is intelligent design. For us, design is about thinking, sharing ideas, rolling up our shirtsleeves, getting on a plane, testing ideas to make sure they actually work. Our research doesn't just take us all over the world; it keeps us there. From team-trekking across Thailand and transport-testing in Toronto, to intelligence-gathering in Geneva and fact-finding on active Australian runways, investigating and integrating are basic tenets of the Winkreative culture. Knowledge is at the heart of all our solutions – it is our strength and the foundation on which we build solid and authentic brand identities.

Express Transformation

Working together since 2011, Union Pearson Express
and Winkreative are building an air-rail link service that
will transform Toronto's transport landscape. President
Kathy Haley describes what's in store.

Union Pearson Express President Kathy Haley says UP Express will go beyond a mere airport shuttle service, to provide Toronto residents and visitors with a "world-class guest experience". Designed to seamlessly link Toronto's largest transport hubs and ease city congestion, UP Express will deliver a robust infrastructure, readying Toronto for the future.

Winkreative
How has the transport landscape in Toronto and Ontario changed in the last decade?

Kathy
More than anything else, what has changed is the population density and demographics of the Greater Toronto and Hamilton Area, or GTHA. We've grown in leaps and bounds, and immigration has been a huge influence along with the growth of businesses and the condo boom. As a result, traffic congestion in Toronto has become a major issue, rivalling that of Los Angeles.

Metrolinx and its subsidiaries have been working hard to get ahead of these changes to create a mobility system across the province that will take us into the future, but we're going to need continued public investment and the support of our communities to accomplish this.

Winkreative
Connectivity to and from the airport is paramount to a city's infrastructure. What was the mandate for UP Express?

Kathy
UP's mandate is to provide Toronto with a world-class guest experience connecting the airport to downtown in time for 2015, when the city hosts the Pan/Parapan American Games.

Winkreative
How important is an efficient transport system to the infrastructure, functioning and well-being of a city?

Kathy
It's crucial. By connecting Toronto's two largest transport hubs, Union Station and Pearson International Airport, the service will bring the world to Toronto. This new, seamless link between air travel and the Greater Toronto Area's local transport infrastructure will be a boon for Toronto's global competitiveness, unlock new economic potential throughout the GTA and deliver a more sustainable, future-ready transport system.

UP Express will also generate substantial benefits for the residents and commuters of the GTA. At present, travelling to and from Pearson Airport by taxi or car service can be expensive and time-unpredictable. The new air-rail link will provide a cost-effective alternative, while the journey time of 25 minutes will save business travellers valuable time.

Winkreative
Why is UP different from other airport shuttle services?

Kathy
We've given the environment design a strong sense of place. We believe the design of the new stations is very strong and projects a clear Ontario sensibility.

We are building a strong service culture so people using the service feel supported throughout every aspect of their journey. That could mean a practical ticket purchase or an unexpected moment to discover a unique product or taste some of the quality goods produced here in the province.

The journey itself is also quite exceptional. While we focus on a seamless passenger journey that has speed and convenience at its core, there are many aspects of the experience that are quite memorable. For example, the dramatic view towards Toronto from the airport platform, or the dynamic stretch of track that starts high up in the terminal and sweeps down towards the city or Union Station, where we have an interesting retail and lounge offer that delivers an exceptional level of comfort in transit.

Winkreative
In terms of international air-rail link standards, how does easing congestion at a city level work with putting Toronto on the world stage?

Kathy
Congestion is a deterrent to people wanting to visit any city. Demonstrating that a city has a robust infrastructure to ensure the mobility of visitors and our own citizens is a strong influence on the reputation and perception of any city. If we can create a positive impression as people arrive in or depart from Toronto, then we will have made a significant contribution towards the global view of Toronto.

The projected increases in congestion show just how serious the threat could be to our city. We have to look at solutions before it escalates to the suffocating levels that some cities currently suffer from. The impact on the economy and the quality of life in the city should not be underestimated.

Winkreative
What does UP Express mean for Toronto?

Kathy
We join a global community of air-rail link services that exist at a high level of quality in cities like London, Tokyo,

Oslo, Vienna and Stockholm. We demonstrate the value we place on being connected to the rest of the world.

UP Express shows the ambition we have for design excellence in transport and hospitality in our province. It creates more options for the people of Toronto, offering a faster connection to the airport, saving on taxi costs or avoiding the inconvenience of asking family or friends to drop you off.

Winkreative
Beyond the Pan American and Parapan American Games, what are the continuing aims of UP?

Kathy
We want to become the preferred way of travelling between the airport and downtown. Also, we want to continually improve and evolve, surprising our guests with the quality of our service and playing a role in showcasing interesting people, places and products from Toronto.

Winkreative
What were you looking for from Winkreative?

Kathy
We went through an extensive competitive procurement process and were looking for a team who appreciated our ambitions for the project, who brought a global perspective to the design direction and had an obsessive attitude towards creating quality travel experiences.

I had seen the work for Porter Airlines and became very interested in the idea of working with the agency that had created their experience. Many aspects of the project were well under way, such as the vehicle design and station architecture, so the ability to collaborate with our operational teams and partners was critical. I had read a lot of Tyler's views about travel and found that we had similar views about the importance of service, design and a sense of place in the passenger journey. I felt he really understood how to capture the sense of pride we have about our province.

Winkreative
What does the Winkreative aesthetic lend to UP?

Kathy
Wink's design work expresses a dignity that seems increasingly absent from the travel experience, yet the work always seems new and modern. That balance of a graceful yet progressive style is central to the UP Express design.

Winkreative
How does the design scheme embrace the materials of the region?

Kathy
A lot of the inspiration from the start came from Ontario's natural resources. So for colour inspiration and materials, we looked at the Ontario timber industry, the Canadian Shield and the Ontario mining sector to inform our direction.

Winkreative
In what ways does UP's identity reflect Canada's spirit?

Kathy
At its heart, the UP identity – the name, logo and secondary elements – all reflect an optimistic, cheerful and welcoming spirit that we think embodies what's best about Canada. The simplicity and directness of the name, with its total lack of pretension, that too reflects the spirit of Canada. At the same time, we've achieved an elegance and originality with the identity that I think will resonate with both local and international customers who are used to executive class travel.

Winkreative
Why do you think you are in our "Intelligence" chapter?

Kathy
We have put great effort into understanding our future customer base. We have also assembled an impressive group of experts for the project, including our organisation and our partners. Our approach combines market intelligence with execution by a focused group of partners. We hope this ensures we deliver a service that feels like the smart choice for our guests.

Our team also sits within a large and established organisational structure, so appreciating the assets of the combined culture and experience is vital to the successful delivery of the air-rail link.

Winkreative
What have been the most effective ways of communicating the UP Express brand and experience? Is there still life in print?

Kathy
We believe that all media have their appropriate use. At the prelaunch stage we've created materials that evoke the vision of the air-rail link and express the viewpoints of a variety of Torontonians about the proposed service. We are using both online and print tools to target different audiences with appropriate information to engage them with our vision.

Winkreative
A great transport system should be...

Kathy
Seamless, serene and elevated.

Union Pearson Express

Country
Canada

Work
**Identity
Digital design
Environment**

Devised by the Ontario transport agency Metrolinx to operate in time for the 2015 Pan/Parapan American Games, the Union Pearson Express (or UP Express) is a long-awaited air-rail link running between Canada's two busiest transport hubs, Union Station and Toronto Pearson International Airport. The link is a major project for the city and will demonstrate Toronto's increasing competitiveness on the global stage.

Winkreative is undertaking all creative work for this important addition to Toronto's transport infrastructure, including the name, design of carriage livery and interiors and, with Hosoya Schaefer Architects, creative direction of the architecture for the four stations along the route. The distinctive colour palette was inspired by the forests, seasons and landscapes of Ontario, helping create an appropriately Canadian welcome to the city of Toronto.

A – ILLUSTRATION
The train on its way
to Toronto Pearson
International Airport.

A

UP Union Pearson Express

A – IDENTITY
The name UP has connotations with an elevated experience, demonstrated by the raised lettering system of the logo.

B – BESPOKE ALPHABET
The lettering harks back to the vintage age of rail, while the arrow devices create a sense of travelling upwards.

OPPOSITE – PATTERN
Bespoke pattern design.

A B C D E
F G H I J
K L M N O
P Q R S T
U V W X Y
Z ⤴ → ↑

A

PREVIOUS PAGES –
PHOTOGRAPHY
Winkreative art-directed
a photographic world that
presents an elevated view
to capture the scale of
the infrastructure project
and the vision of a future
Toronto.

A – INTERIORS
Train interiors
incorporate the arrow
visual device, fabrics,
carpet specifications
and embroidered leather
headrest covers as
advised by Winkreative.

B, C – ENVIRONMENT
Proposed interiors
of Toronto Pearson
International Airport
and Union Station,
incorporating signage
and ticket machines,
designed by Winkreative.

B

A

A – ANIMATION
An animation explains UP's proposed service.

B – FILM
Stills from a film produced to communicate Toronto's need for an air-rail link, including interviews with locals.

B

In Modern Thailand

The Government of Thailand is laying the groundwork to ensure sustained – and sustainable – economic growth and an optimistic future for the country and its people.

What matters more to success – ambition or talent? Surely one without the other is useless. Fortunately, Thailand has an abundance of both. Thanks to an ambitious government programme, plans are under way to use the kingdom's talents to its advantage and push the country forward.

The government is spending US$67 billion on an infrastructure programme to improve transportation, encourage creativity and support its growing industries, thereby increasing the all-round efficiency of the country and improving the quality of life for its own population, international visitors and its Association of Southeast Asian Nations (ASEAN) neighbours. By realising all it has to offer, Thailand is now laying the groundwork to ensure its growth is sustained and its talent nurtured, in order to become a thoroughly modern nation.

For booming business and tourism industries, connectivity is key. Investing in high-speed rail – laying 50 per cent more track than what is currently in place – will connect key northern hubs such as Chiang Mai with the financial clout of the capital, and the south. Upgrades to the intra-city mass transit systems will boost trade, slashing the cost of transporting the country's plentiful commodities; while a state-of-the-art rail network will create better connections for the rapid shuttling of people and goods. US$11.9 billion is being spent on roads, and construction of the Friendship Bridges – designed to better connect Thailand with its neighbours Laos,

Malaysia and Myanmar – is surging forward. International connectivity, which starts at the airport, will also be improved, thanks to a three-year upgrade of the country's main airport, Suvarnabhumi, which currently accommodates 53 million people annually.

Improving connectivity has positive knock-on effects for almost every aspect of Thai life. Increasing local social mobility enables families to live together, rather than parents moving into the cities for work while grandparents raise children in more affordable areas. The government is building and investing widely – convention centres to attract businesses, advanced factories to increase manufacturing capabilities and productivity (investment in renewables such as solar energy and eco-cars is particularly high) and Thailand Science Park, which groups companies and researchers to foster innovation through proximity.

The food industry is also seeing radical innovation through the active promotion of sustainable organic agriculture. The government has set up the Industrial Technology Assistance Programme to provide farmers with training and advice on how to adapt their farms to organic production, so Thai farmers can keep up with the demand for pesticide-free produce from both Thailand's own market and those overseas, and therefore see a slice of the US$100 billion-plus annual global organic market that is steadily growing.

Thailand's creative industry is another area successfully generating its own economy, and the government is investing in its continued development. Initiatives such as Handmade Chiang Mai – a British Council-Chiang Mai University union – encourage creative partnerships with other nations.

Thailand is thriving. In the past two decades, its economy has grown each year by an average of 4 per cent, and now, with a strong infrastructure plan in place, Thailand can support continued growth. The multi-pronged approach, using both short- and long-term policies in four key areas, will ensure that Thailand is ready to take on the future and cement its position as a regional and global powerhouse.

PREVIOUS PAGE
Suvarnabhumi Airport;
architect, designer and
critic Duangrit Bunnag.

ABOVE
Friends enjoy a glass
alongside the vines at
Siam Winery.

The Government of Thailand

Country
Thailand
Work
Strategy
Identity
Digital design
Publishing
Advertising
Environment
Film

As Thailand prepared to host the 2012 World Economic Forum on East Asia, Winkreative was selected by the Office of the Prime Minister to promote the country's many assets and ambitious plans for growth.

After devising a long-term communications strategy, we created an identity that captures Thailand's modern spirit, revealing a sense of drive and purpose and a progressive, cosmopolitan outlook.

A global advertising campaign was the next task, for which Winkreative developed concepts, copy and epic photography. The print executions, which focus on four key messages, have appeared in internationally respected titles, including the *Financial Times*, the *International Herald Tribune* and *The Economist*, as well as on prominent billboards throughout Bangkok. The campaign is designed to serve as an umbrella brand for the whole of Thailand, evolving over time and expanding to incorporate additional aspects of the government, economy and society.

A – IDENTITY
The bold black logo is a modern and confident statement. Thai character is added in the T and "d", which creates a solid framing device.

B – MARQUE
Inspired by the local Thai elephants. The marque is a deconstruction of the national identity.

C – ICONS
The icons symbolise the different sectors of the government programme and are used as navigation tools in print and online.

A

Thailand

B

C

Thailand

MANUFACTURE

DRIVING THE FUTURE

The elephant isn't Thailand's only low-emission form of transport – in fact, we've become one of the world's top producers of eco-cars since, recognising a powerful opportunity, the government launched a determined policy to encourage investment. Now, drawn by our skilled workforce, engineering expertise and business friendly incentives, big names like Mitsubishi, Suzuki and Honda are making their next-generation, sustainable cars here that will steer the global automotive future.

Visit Modern-Thailand.com

Thailand

TRADE

FIRST PORT OF CALL

At Laem Chabang, one of the world's busiest seaports, it's easy to see why Thailand is such a dynamic trading hub within the region and across the seas. Entrepreneurial by nature and boasting a multi-skilled workforce, we're busy making sure that vital goods get to market on time, every time. With the fourth-lowest unemployment rate in the world, it's our hands-on approach that's made us the globe's fifth-largest container-shipping nation.

Visit Modern-Thailand.com

Thailand

CULTURE

ร้านคุณยุ
จำหน่ายผักสดผลไม้ อาหารปรุงสุก

GLOBAL KITCHEN

Thai food is loved around the world, but few people know that Thailand boasts as many distinct cuisines as it does regions. In Chiang Mai, this means an artful blend of influences from China, Laos and Myanmar, featuring unique ingredients like native strawberries, simply eaten in season with salt, sugar and chilli. Grown in enviably fertile soils, Thailand's abundance of fresh produce is skilfully turned into halal street snacks or five-star dining, each mouthful telling the fascinating, edible and ongoing history of each town and region. Discover a delicious new side to modern Thailand.

Visit Modern-Thailand.com

FULL SPEED AHEAD

Modern Thailand is on the move. Take transport: we're investing heavily in our rail network, from urban mass-transit systems to a new US$26 billion high-speed rail link that will criss-cross the country – taking rubber from plantation to port, and tourists from Bangkok to beach, faster than ever before, generating growth in all corners of the country. We've even developed a solar-powered prototype of our famous tuk-tuks, for a cleaner, greener urban journey. Welcome to fast-lane Thailand.

Visit Modern-Thailand.com

Thailand

INFRASTRUCTURE

MAKING TRACKS

As well as producing more of the world's rubber than any other country, Thailand is also the place where it's turned into peerless products – including superior handmade Specialized tyres that propel many Tour de France cyclists across the finish line. With Thailand's rich supplies of the raw material, advanced manufacturing facilities, excellent incentives for business and expert, multi-skilled technicians, it's little wonder that some of the world's best-known brands, from Michelin to Challenge, come here to get things rolling.

Visit Modern-Thailand.com

B

PREVIOUS PAGES –
ADVERTISING
The overall idea for
the campaign was
to change people's
preconceptions of
Thailand. The copy
plays on perceptions
and conveys surprising
facts to send a positive,
new message. The
photography evokes
a sense of scale and
growth, but also
humanity.

A – ANIMATION
Focusing on the
infrastructure campaign,
this animated TV
commercial, broadcast
across international
news channels in 15-,
30- and 60-second spots,
is a vision of Thailand's
connected future.

B – MAGAZINE COVER
A composite cover
reflects Thailand's key
economic areas.

C – SPREADS
Portrait photography
creates an intimacy with
the people, while large-
scale, pulled-back
shots evoke aspirations
for the future.

NEXT PAGES –
ILLUSTRATION AND
PHOTOGRAPHY
The magazine employed
mainly Thai talent, such
as local illustrators and
photographers.

C

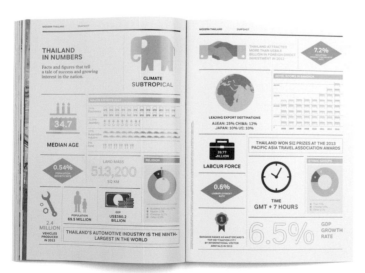

Intelligence guides our global industry research
providing a solid foundation on which to build a brand.

Projects
Mackintosh | GO Transit
Brisbane Airport Corporation
Grosvenor Ltd

Client
Mackintosh

Country
United Kingdom

Work
Publishing
Packaging

Winkreative found a kindred spirit in British heritage brand Mackintosh. As it launched its first flagship store on London's Mount Street, we took the opportunity to indulge in the kind of obsessive detail for which Mackintosh itself is famed.

Winkreative designed the packaging, including swing tags, custom ribbon, receipt folders and shop cards as well as the luxurious brown bag: heavy uncoated paper, waxed on the reverse for water resistance and stability,

with an embossed silk-screened logo and a black cotton herringbone ribbon handle – a nod to the in-store parquetry – with its own Japanese-style rain protector in case of showers.

To celebrate all things Mackintosh, a limited-edition broadsheet was also created, making its debut at the Winkreative-organised London launch party and becoming available afterwards at key stores globally.

A

A – LAUNCH MATERIALS
The packaging for the UK store launch included a silk-screened, embossed waxed-paper bag with a herringbone ribbon handle and a protective rainproof cover.

OPPOSITE – PATTERN
A pattern created from elements of St Andrew's cross.

NEXT PAGE –
BROADSHEET
A newspaper detailing the history of the brand and the manufacturing process was distributed at the launch of the London store.

Client
GO Transit

Country
Canada

Work
**Identity
Environment**

A division of Metrolinx, GO is the regional public transit service for the Greater Toronto and Hamilton Area. Well known and respected among Ontarians, GO serves 65 million passengers a year.

A major renovation of Toronto's Union Station was the catalyst to modernise the external expression of the GO brand. Winkreative initiated an identity update, revitalising the logo, livery and interiors and specifying new communication standards through a series of

marketing materials, Union Station signage, brand graphics and printed materials, such as posters, newsletters and timetables. These detailed guidelines will dictate all future applications for GO Transit.

To support the local architects assigned to each station, Winkreative worked with the team at Hosoya Schaefer Architects to provide an overarching design direction, thereby ensuring that a continuous visual language is extended throughout the passenger experience.

A

A – LOGO
The refreshed logo is easy to apply at a range of scales, while the strong green palette is consistent with the Metrolinx family.

A

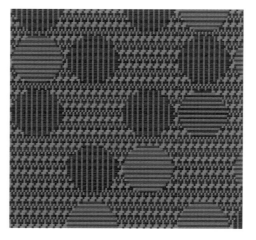

A – INTERIORS
Bespoke fabrics were
commissioned as
part of the vehicle
interior design.

B, PREVIOUS PAGES –
LIVERY
A lighter colour palette
is used for the livery,
which, in its simplicity,
will continue to express
the GO brand as it
evolves.

OPPOSITE – ILLUSTRATION
The vision poster is a
visual expression of the
strategy, reflecting the
optimism of GO.

B

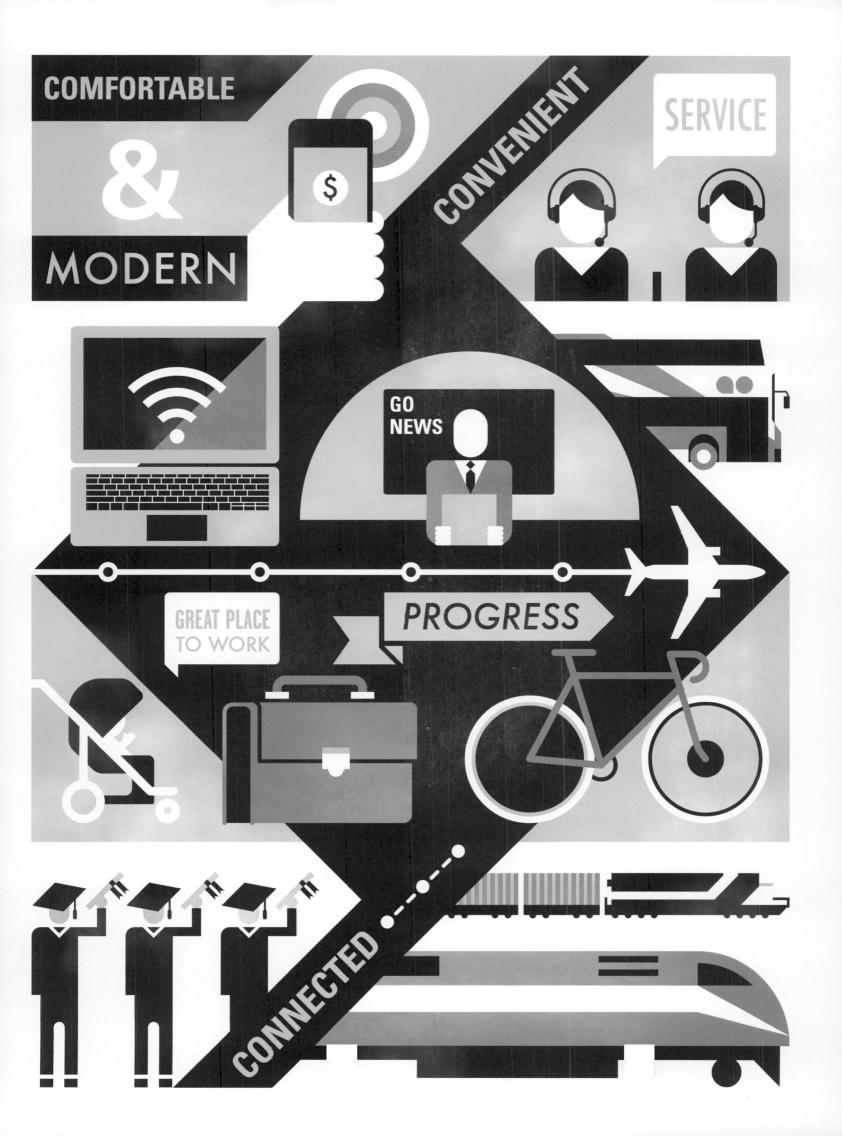

Client
**Brisbane Airport
Corporation**

Country
Australia

Work
**Strategy
Identity
Publishing**

As part of an extensive strategy and identity piece for Brisbane Airport, Winkreative produced a 76-page brand book, presenting the vision for a new era for Australia's third-busiest airport. Featuring arresting illustration, photography and art direction, *Going Places: A Blueprint for Brisbane Airport* provides a fitting insight into the future of this airport hub.

A

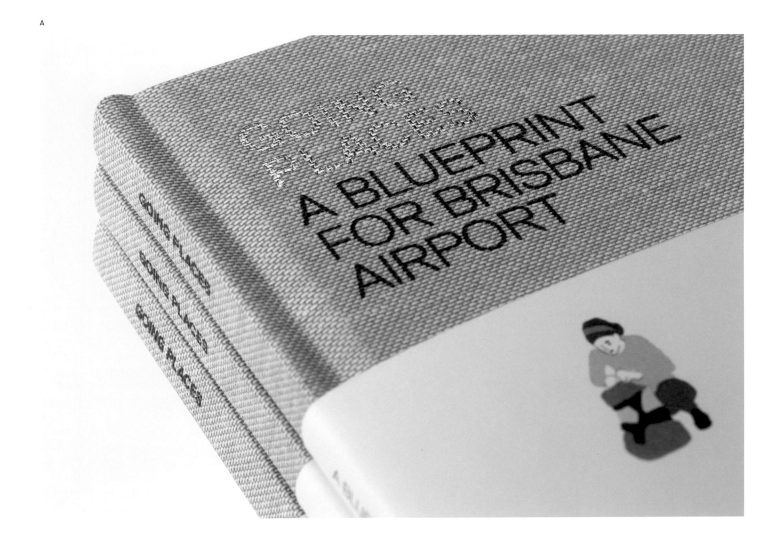

B

C

A

A,D — ILLUSTRATION
Strong illustrations
by Asako Masunouchi
are used on divider
pages, helping represent
each section and
contextualise the project.

B,C — SPREADS
The aerial shot of the
airport is a natural leader
into the book; colourful
infographics highlight
relevant statistics.

B

C

D

Client
Grosvenor Ltd
Country
Hong Kong
Work
Identity
Publishing

Operated by the prestigious property developer Grosvenor Ltd, The Westminster is a high-end apartment building in Tokyo's affluent residential area of Roppongi Hills.

Winkreative was commissioned to devise a complete identity for the project, conveying Grosvenor's vision to create the highest standards of modern living combined with a commitment to sustainable luxury and the careful custodianship of local craft and culture.

Winkreative designed a logo and identity centred around elegance and understated luxury. A book was produced in support, exploring the area, profiling international architects and introducing the local artisans who were commissioned to create the site-specific artworks for The Westminster's communal areas.

A

THE
WESTMINSTER
ROPPONGI

PREVIOUS PAGE A –
IDENTITY
The marque was inspired by the floor plans of The Westminster tower, playing with the idea of elevation. The layered W device gives a sense of height and growth.

PREVIOUS PAGE B –
PHOTOGRAPHY
The day and night photography helps readers experience the building at both times, while maps of the entire city and the local neighbourhood emphasise the proximity to local restaurants, bars, retail and schools.

OPPOSITE –
PHOTOGRAPHY
Winkreative commissioned and art-directed photography of the development.

A – BOXED BOOK
The logo on the cloth-covered box is depicted in copper foil, while the interior silk-screened pattern was generated from the logo.

B – SPREAD
Interviews with collaborators such as local stone artist Masatoshi Izumi, who created site-specific sculptures for The Westminster, offer insight into the residence from a cultural perspective.

A

B

Clarity

The easiest story to tell is often the real one. The identity of a brand is, in essence, its message, and a good way to explain this message clearly is to seek out and tell the truth. The simplicity of Swiss International Air Lines, the integrity of Avenue Road, the unwavering manifesto of *The Calvert Journal,* the fortitude of USM Holdings – take the truth behind the brand and let it drive honest, efficient communications. As designers and storytellers, we have a tendency to overdesign and overcomplicate – to do too much – when often the simplest solution is the right one. Intuition is key, self-restraint often called for, and once you start communicating, absolute confidence in the single message is essential. You can't imitate authenticity.

The Russian
Cultural Revolution

Founded by Nonna Materkova, Calvert 22 is a charitable
foundation raising awareness of contemporary Russian culture.
Winkreative has collaborated with Materkova to create
The Calvert Journal and cement the brand on many platforms.

Founded by Nonna Materkova, *The Calvert Journal* aims to improve Russia's image through culture and art. By bringing the unfamiliar territory of contemporary Russia into the spotlight and giving a voice to a rising generation of young artistic talent, the journal hopes to change perceptions and reinstate Russia as a leading cultural and intellectual hub.

Winkreative
What do you think is the perception of modern Russia?

Nonna
Unfortunately, I don't think it's very bright. I have a subjective, more positive view, but if you live in the UK, for example, you know that Russia is not perceived well. Old Russia is well known, and the greats, such as Pushkin, Dostoyevsky, Chekhov, the National Ballet and Russian classical music, are admired, but modern culture is not well known at all. In the UK particularly, Russians are seen as flashy, tasteless people covered in gold and diamonds, but this isn't my Russia at all, because I can see different things. There are lots of young, talented people who have brilliant, creative ideas and want integration into the international world. This is what we want to do here.

Winkreative
How have perceptions changed over the last decade?

Nonna
It's up and down. Lots of Russians now live in London and abroad. These people are well educated and bring a positive message. It's getting better, but there's still a lot of work ahead to change perceptions of contemporary Russia.

Winkreative
Why did you feel you needed to form Calvert?

Nonna
I'm from St Petersburg, which is the cultural capital of Russia. I've always gone to museums and been interested in classical culture, but when I came to London 13 years ago, I became fascinated with contemporary art and started going to openings, studios, the Frieze art fair; I wanted to investigate this area in Russia. Then I found this space in London's vibrant area of Shoreditch and thought I'd like to do something with it, so it all grew from there. As an economist, I've always invested, and building a platform to promote positive perceptions of Russia through cultural works seems like the best investment yet.

Winkreative
How does Calvert work on a logistical level?

Nonna
It's certainly a project that requires networks – it's citizen journalism – so in all the different regions of Russia, which is still the biggest country in the world, we are growing a network of bloggers and people who contribute using social media. We have an editorial team of eight people in London, who are all young, smart and connected to contemporary culture, so through them we are growing our network. Our Russian team sorts through the projects that come in, which can be hundreds in a day because Russian people are so hungry to be heard, and selects projects to present to the British team. The idea is to pick up on what's relevant for the international audience. It's hard work, but it's very exciting, and when you see that you've helped give a voice to a person somewhere in the middle of Russia, it's wonderful.

Winkreative
How do you think the Russian government perceives this?

Nonna
Well, we're not dependent on the government at all, because I started the foundation. I'm very passionate about it, and we are trying to be independent. What I've learned is that if you're doing something you're passionate about, which is interesting to other people, then people will come to support you. Now we have investment from one of Russia's largest investment banks and a partnership with Alexei Kudrin, the dean of the Department of Liberal Arts and Sciences at St Petersburg State University. 2014 is the UK/Russia Year of Culture, in which we'll certainly take part, and we'll be noticed without government help.

Winkreative
Why did you choose Wink to help you on your journey?

Nonna
Somehow, I'm always following what Tyler is doing. I like what he did with *Wallpaper* and now *Monocle*, so after we met, I knew he was what we needed. I think he's a genius, and his team is both international and articulate. Everything Winkreative does is thoughtful, down to the very last detail, but it's also about the process and how everything actually works. That was very attractive to us, and people always comment on the visual part of the brand, so we're very honoured.

Winkreative
How did the Calvert brand in your mind compare with the one Winkreative presented? What were you expecting?

Nonna
I didn't have any expectations in my mind. We didn't articulate anything visually; we just wanted to see something edgy and contemporary, but distinguished and different. It was a very exciting moment! There was no struggle at all. We were shown two routes, and at the first one, the whole team said, "This is it!" – it was unanimous. It looked like a stamp, a bold statement, which we liked very much, but there's also something about the lines, the colour and the craft aspect that transmits equality and opportunity. There was no doubt in my mind that it was absolutely right for us.

Old Russia is well known, and the greats, such as Pushkin, Dostoyevsky and Chekhov are admired, but modern culture is not well known at all.

Winkreative
What has Winkreative enabled you to do?

Nonna
It's enabled us to be an international brand. What we didn't want to see is something that brings up Russian stereotypes. Yes, it's creativity from Russia, but it doesn't need that geographical limitation: if art is good, then it's universally good. The identity is unique; in fact, lots of people have commented that they've never seen anything like this from Russia before. We wanted to step away from saying that Russia is powerful, and present the human face of Russia, one that is in some ways very ordinary, but in terms of all the talented people who don't have a voice, not ordinary at all. Winkreative has given us the ability to share this abundance of talent.

Winkreative
You are a platform for art and culture. Can culture exist independently of politics?

Nonna
I think it cannot completely avoid politics – particularly contemporary art, which is grounded in social and political issues. However, what I've really started to notice is that young Russian people are not necessarily interested in politics – they want to realise themselves and want their ideas to be implemented, so this is what we're trying to do.

Winkreative
What is your view of the role of magazines, and how much of an influence do you think they can have?

Nonna
I think there's still life and influence in print – the magazine has become an iconic feature in modern culture – but for what we do, an online magazine makes a lot more sense, because it's easier to reach people and distribute the information. We're also a not-for-profit organisation, so an online approach makes financial sense, but people still like to have something tangible to hold, so we printed a launch publication. This was a digest of sorts, which included some highlights from the website. Now we're thinking of doing this twice a year, because it looked and felt great!

Winkreative
Which artist, designer or cultural figure inspires you?

Nonna
I should say that when I see the incredible creativity of Russia, I couldn't just identify one person. It's a whole energy coming from all the disparate parts of the country, and it's an enormous privilege to work with this sort of energy and do something helpful for it. Having said that, Tyler Brûlé is very much my icon – and I'm not just saying that! Honestly, he has an amazing vision, and I absolutely admire everything he does. It was a privilege to work with the company.

Winkreative
What's next? What's the future of Calvert 22?

Nonna
Well, we only launched six months ago, so we're still babies! I can see huge interest from all over the world – we have major audiences in the UK, the US and Russia, and we also have amazing cliques in Afghanistan, Iran, Peru, Mali – countries we never thought we could reach! Who knows what will happen in the future, but I'm very excited.

Calvert 22 Foundation

Country
United Kingdom

Work
**Identity
Publishing
Digital design**

The Calvert Journal is a daily briefing on the culture and creativity of modern Russia. Winkreative designed the website for the launch, which provides regular updates on art, design, film, architecture and culture through an engaging mix of reportage, interviews, profiles and reviews.

We also developed an encompassing brand strategy to cement *The Calvert Journal*'s position as the pre-eminent source for contemporary Russian culture, and conceived a logo and colour palette to be implemented across various applications and platforms.

A – LOGO
Inspired by the journal's multifaceted approach, the numerous lines represent the many cultural areas that *The Calvert Journal* covers on a daily basis.

A

RUSSIA

THE
CALVERT JOURNAL
—
A GUIDE TO
CREATIVE RUSSIA

A

ILLUSTRATION
A map of Russia's
defining cultural
districts.

OPPOSITE – COVER
The cover has a foil-
embossed logo, and the
buckram-embossed
paper mimics that of
old journals.

A – SPREADS
Each section features
Q&As, locally
commissioned
photography and
interviews with thought
leaders in the arts and
culture field for each city.

A

56 NOVOSIBIRSK

57

GRAND DESIGNS

Architect Fyodor Bukhtoyarov has plans on Novosibirsk's skyline

TEXT *Olga Zavarzina*
PHOTOGRAPHY *Anton Unitsyn/Grinberg Agency*

When he first started out, architect and designer Fyodor Bukhtoyarov was not an instant hit. His oversized chandeliers and glass bottle walls were too outlandish for the inhabitants of Novosibirsk, most of whom preferred neutral spaces. A decade later and it is Bukhtoyarov who is setting the style agenda. By sticking to an aesthetic that is vivid, playful and always individual, he has won round the doubters and established himself as the most prominent creative force on Siberia's urban landscape.

Today, clients are willing to fork out vast sums for his creative input. Bukhtoyarov has designed interiors and exteriors for restaurants, cafes, nightclubs and shops. His portfolio even boasts shopping centres and the terminal of an international airport. In the process, he's done more than any single recent figure to introduce a distinctive visual identity to a part of Russia that's been mostly bypassed by good design.

For the past 20 years, Novosibirsk has undergone a process of dramatic transformation, swapping its Soviet industrial heritage for a cul-

ture of commerce. Sombre factories have turned into shopping centres, sleepy suburbs are now overrun with malls and high-rise developments are springing up across the city centre. Sweeping gentrification has resulted in a uniformity of design throughout the city.

For most property developers, architectural artistry is not a great concern – flats sell at astronomical prices regardless of what they look like. This indifference, and interference from clients in large-scale projects, is one reason why Bukhtaryov would like to focus on interiors and objects. "I would like to lock myself in my studio and design a chair," he says. "Then there would be no one telling me what to do."

Despite such frustrations, Bukhtoyarov takes a rueful pleasure in the city's evolution. His office is situated in the least developed part of Krasny Prospekt, Novosibirsk's main thoroughfare, with windows looking out onto an impressive Stalin-era facade complete with crumbling columns. Everything on this stretch of the road is as it was 60 years ago. From there he reflects on the city's changing skyline, the monolithic Soviet blocks of old jostling uncomfortably with modern new builds.

Bukhtoyarov describes Novosibirsk's development as a "story frozen in time, a sort of elemental Siberian mosaic". "That is why I like these shocking new builds, even though many people attack them for 'sticking out' against the general background of the grey Soviet buildings," he says. "These different eras accentuate each other and make the city unique."

According to Bukhtoyarov, one of the consequences of this new style of architectural homogeneity is that people end up looking for other ways to set themselves apart. "People here, if they want to show how well-off they are, invest their money in an expensive car or in jewellery from Bulgari," he says. "I think it's because everyone's home is more or less the same so with your car or your clothes you can really stand out."

LEFT PAGE
Bukhtoyarov in his studio in Novosibirsk

TOP
Bukhtoyarov's studio is situated in Novosibirsk's main thoroughfare

FYODOR BUKHTOYAROV'S
TOP NOVOSIBIRSK ARCHITECTURAL SITES

Salt
Nordic-style restaurant serving European, Russian and Asian food

Cocoon Business Centre
Striking convex glass building in a drab business district. Built in 2011

Killer Bar
The way in to this 1950s New York loft-style bar is through a red shipping container

Beerman & Pelmeni
Restaurant specialising in beer and dumplings from around the world. Shelves of matryoshka dolls accent a minimalist interior

College of Chemistry
Built in 1932, this is one of the best examples of Constructivist architecture in Novosibirsk

House with a Clock
Constructivist apartment block designed by celebrated architect Nikolai Nikitin in the 1930s

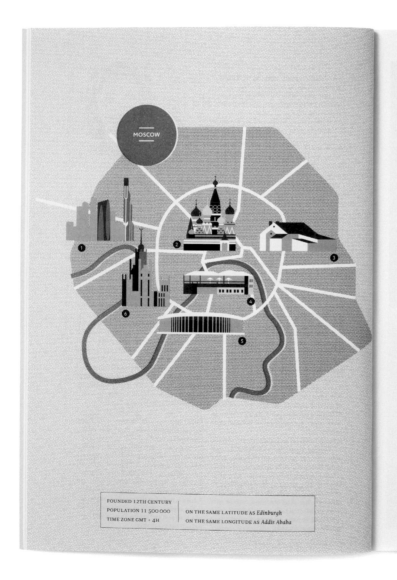

MOSCOW

11

MOSCOW
—

Even for the 200 years when it wasn't the capital, Moscow has always been the heart of Russia.

But it's an international city too; its check-shirted hipsters and power-dressed execs look more to Manhattan than Murmansk.

Combining the global reach of digital media with local invention, Moscow's ambitious creatives are poised to set the tone not just for Russia, but the whole world.

FOUNDED 12TH CENTURY
POPULATION 11 500 000
TIME ZONE GMT + 4H

ON THE SAME LATITUDE AS *Edinburgh*
ON THE SAME LONGITUDE AS *Addis Ababa*

CITY HIGHLIGHTS

MOSCOW CITY
Business district still under construction with a number of skyscrapers due to be completed by 2015 (1)

MOSCOW METRO
One of Russia's most ornate architectural projects and significant engineering achievements. Opened in 1935

ST BASIL'S CATHEDRAL
Ultimate symbol of Russia on Red Square (2)

MAYAKOVSKY MUSEUM
Home to an eclectic collection of sketches and writings of Soviet poet Vladimir Mayakovsky

WINZAVOD
Former bottling factory that now houses a cluster of leading contemporary art galleries and high-end boutiques (3)

RODNYA STUDIO
Art gallery, lecture hall, design studio, bar, cinema and nightclub in a 19th-century former factory

STRELKA INSTITUTE
Multifunctional, not-for-profit educational centre with a popular bar and terrace that attracts top names in design and urban planning to its series of public lectures, conferences and film screenings (4)

GARAGE CENTRE FOR CONTEMPORARY ART
Not-for-profit arts centre founded by Dasha Zhukova in 2008. Moved to Gorky Park in 2012 (5)

CHISTYE PRUDY
Picturesque pond with paddle boats in the summer and a skating rink in the winter

SEVEN SISTERS
Group of seven Stalinist-style skyscrapers built after WWII (6)

GORKY PARK
Soviet park revamped in 2011 with an ice rink, an open-air cinema, a cafe and gallery space

A – SPREADS
The journal features five Russian cities, with each introduced by an illustrated map. The grainy texture recalls Russian constructivist posters of the 1920s and 1930s.

OPPOSITE – ILLUSTRATION
The key attributes of each city are referenced by playful symbols.

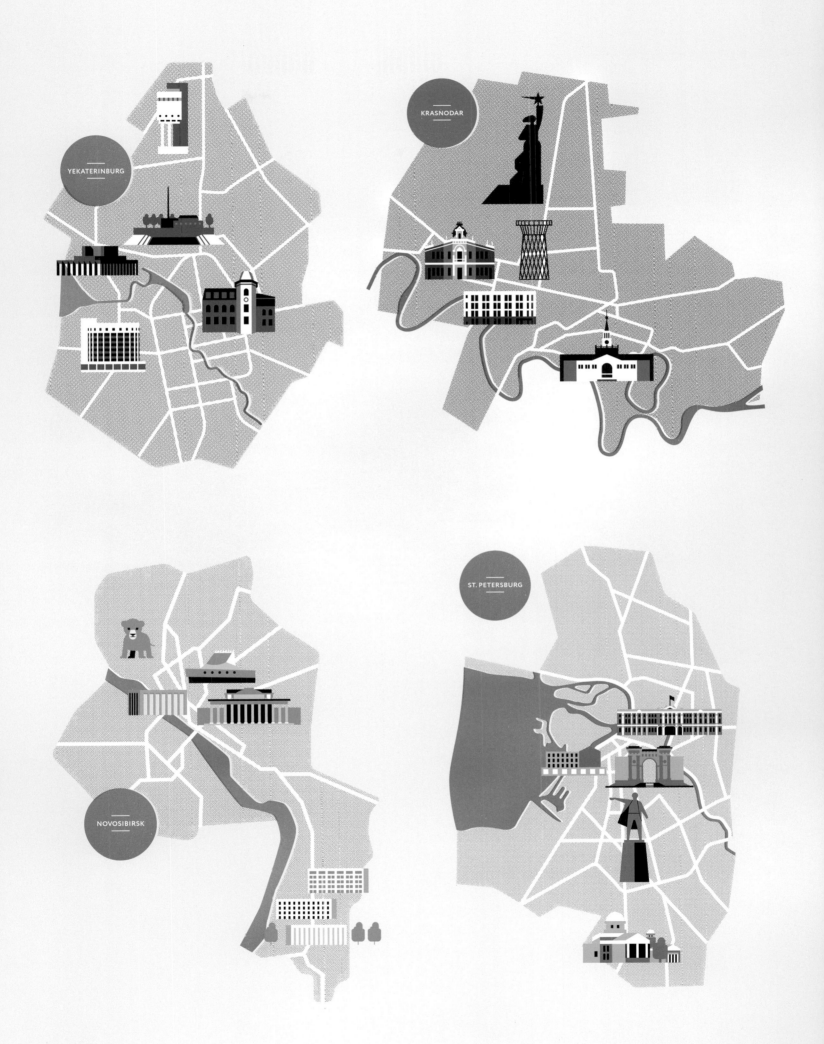

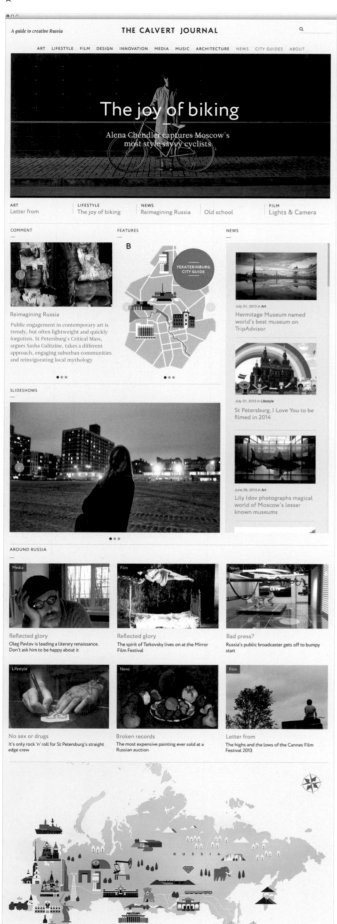

Close encounter: how an American expat became Moscow's foremost cheesemaker

28 May 2013 · More articles

♀ Moscow

US-born Jay Robert Close has lived in Mexico, Australia and Bora-Bora. But it is in the depths of the Russian countryside that he has finally settled and it is cheese that he devotes his time to

Text: Dmitry Panov
Image: Alexei Mikhailovich

Jay Robert Close is a man of many hats. He has in the past fed crocodiles at a farm in Papua New Guinea, built swimming pools, worked as a carpenter and as a driver for a travelling circus. Along the way, Close, who was born in New York and raised in Mexico, has lived in Australia, New Zealand, Fiji, Bora-Bora and Hawaii. He speaks English, French, Italian, Spanish and Russian. After years of a peripatetic lifestyle, the 50-year-old finally settled in Russia. Now he lives in the depths of the Russian countryside where he has devoted himself to cheesemaking.

When he first moved to Russia, it was to Moscow in 2005. After three years of battling with endless traffic jams and locals' brusque attitudes, Close decided to relocate to the Russian hinterland. "I was tired of all that. I wanted to be my own boss," he says. "To build my own home and not depend on anyone." His move to Solnechnogorsk, a village north-west of Moscow, has worked out well. As well as selling cheese, Close has opened up his farm to agritourism. Now anyone who's interested can drop by for a visit. "My house is only 700 metres from the Moscow-St Petersburg main road," he says. "Buses come, tourists visit me, drink milk and tea and buy cheese."

RELATED

Seasonal appeal
Boris Akimov is standing up for real food

"It's never boring in Russia and I'm the sort of guy who needs to be constantly shaken up"

A – WEBSITE
Winkreative designed and built The Calvert Journal website. Updated daily, the home page features the latest articles from five main categories on a carousel, a scrolling news bar, slide shows, reports and weekly mixtapes.

The Editors

Designers and makers from five continents come together at Avenue Road, each with a unique vision and a different story to tell.

Having products by so many design talents under one roof, made from a breadth of materials and expressive of so many different design schools and cultures, could be a recipe for chaos. But thanks to the discerning eye and extraordinary curating skills of founder Stephan Weishaupt, the collection is brilliantly eclectic rather than haphazardly so.

"The most difficult aspect of editing is staying true to our core beliefs and values," says Weishaupt, who started Avenue Road based on the vision that furniture should tell a story from a distinct point of view. "Of course, there are so many great talents, but working with those who share our vision and passion is often the dictating factor."

This has brought forth a collection that not only challenges convention but also encourages people to engage with both the physical object and the entire process behind the design. In the showrooms, acclaimed pieces by industry legends share space with those by

fresh and emerging names, while every product reveals a unique take on materials, colour and technique.

Marlieke Van Rossum's elegant oak furniture is made in the same rural Dutch village where she grew up. "Oak is a force of nature, and we recognise this," she says, and the beautiful simplicity of her designs allows the rich character of the material to speak for itself. Next to rough texture comes smooth and shiny in the form of young-blood Sebastian Herkner's sculptural glass and solid brass Bell tables, made using traditional crafts such as glass-blowing and steam-bending.

Herkner tracked down one of the last specialist glass-blowers in Bavaria, who comes from a 13-generation glass-blowing family, as well as an Italian company adept at traditional wood technologies. "My impetus for working with these artisans is social as well as practical," he says. "It's important to preserve [this] part of our heritage." While Herkner turns commonplace materials into striking shapes, the local Toronto studio of Moss & Lam creates visual poetry with its "Walking Bear" cement sculptures, which pad furtively around Avenue Road's New York showroom, subtly doubling up as side tables.

Contemporary designers such as Italian furniture-maker Massimo Castagna, German product designer Konstantin Grcic, Brazilian woodworker Carlos Motta and Cypriot lighting designer Michael Anastassiades represent Avenue Road's global mix. In an appreciative nod to heritage, Avenue Road also stocks pieces by legendary producers such as the centuries-old Nymphenburg Porcelain and the iconic Brazilian muralist Paulo Werneck, while it recently led a celebrated re-edition of Jacques Guillon's Cord chair.

Spanning the globe and honouring the past and present, the Avenue Road collection is underpinned by an overall commitment to honest, meaningful design. This not only creates an inspiring collection of people, products and stories; it also promises an exciting future.

PREVIOUS PAGE
The Avenue Road showroom in Toronto; Bell tables by Sebastian Herkner.

TOP AND ABOVE
Light Ring by Massimo Castagna; MUC table by Christophe Delcourt.

Avenue Road

Country
Canada

Work
Publishing

Established as a showcase for seductive, sophisticated furniture, Avenue Road has become the premier retailer of classic and contemporary design. Advocating the philosophy that furniture should tell a story from a distinct point of view, the company offers an exclusive range of furniture, lighting and accessories from around the world.

To capture the story behind the company and its designers, Winkreative devised *The Storybook*, which enables Avenue Road to further explore the craft of these global designers and makers. *The Storybook* combines editorial features, profiles of designers, both historical and emerging, and a selection of the interior spaces of Avenue Road's private clients. The purity of the studio still-life and lifestyle photography takes Avenue Road in a new visual direction, focusing on materials, shapes and textures and revealing the beauty and diversity of the products.

The Storybook is both an elegant catalogue and a good read – a tactile, collectible addition to any coffee table.

A – COVER
With its straightforward approach, the cover focuses on the basic architecture, materials and shapes of the designs in the Avenue Road collection.

NEXT PAGES –
PHOTOGRAPHY
"The Edit" combines architectural still-life and lifestyle shots. The section features pieces from the current Avenue Road collection, forming the centrepiece of the catalogue.

A

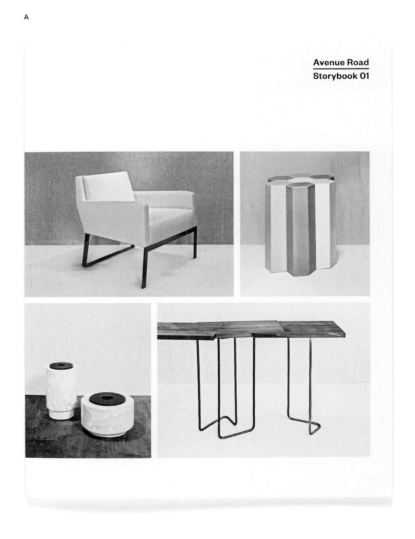

Avenue Road
Storybook 01

Architect and designer Massimo Castagna discusses Italian craftsmanship, respect for the environment and the ethos behind his contemporary furniture collection.

AR: How was the connection forged between you and Avenue Road?

MC: Avenue Road is an important and well-known name in the world of home furnishings, and one of the most interesting dealers in North America. I work very closely with manufacturers in Italy, so we had various European design contacts in common. It was, therefore, a natural connection. Today Avenue Road both treats and distributes products by the furniture design company Henge, for which I'm a designer and art director.

AR: What's the ethos behind your furniture design, and what can we expect from you in the future?

MC: When designing my first collection I thought about how I would furnish my own home, trying to avoid overt styling or designing with the tastes of any particular market in mind. It was a risky approach, but one that paid off, as I hope my designs are unique, imaginative and approachable. I have since achieved a level of international success that is way beyond my initial expectations. It's so satisfactory to see my products chosen to be part of the Avenue Road collection, and by other dealers in all four corners of the globe. Who knows where the next two years will take me?

AR: How do you ensure the highest quality of craftsmanship in your pieces?

MC: Each project starts with a vision or a feeling, and then matures into dedicated research. Form and matter are the most important and expressive elements of a project, and they should be developed simultaneously. Materials have individual characters, and if a material is allowed to express itself fully, then there should be far fewer limitations to the design and production process.

Facing page – Cage B shelving system and Side H cabinet

Right – Light Ring

AR: To what extent does your experience as an architect inform your furniture design?

MC: I studied architecture and graduated in 1984 from Milan's Politecnico. During my years as a student I was educated by some of the great masters of Italian design and architecture. One was Marco Zanuso, a pioneer of postwar Italian design, and another was Cini Boeri, who taught me during my degree thesis. I have always been interested in buildings, but also in interior design, furniture design and art direction. My father had engineered and produced the system Graphis by Tecno in 1968, so design was something I had grown up around.

Ultimately, design and architecture are two disciplines that naturally inform and reciprocate each other. They may be different specializations with different intellectual values, but they are both mirrors of the times, or expressions of modern life. In 1986 I founded the architecture and interior design firm AD Architettura, and began to combine my interests in a professional capacity.

AR: All of your products are made in Italy. What is special or superior about Italian manufacturing?

MC: It's all in the detail, and a certain intellectual capacity or know-how that is part of our DNA. I am proud to be an Italian designer because there are so many master craftsmen and excellent architects and designers that have gone before me.

Exceptionally skilled craft is clearly visible in so much Italian industrial production. When a product has been made with expert hands it has an immediate meaning, a story behind it, a legacy.

AR: What age-old, traditional methods do you use in your work?

MC: There isn't one method in particular that dominates, really. My work moves from an idea to a period of research, and that original idea normally changes and evolves. Nothing is ever obvious, and the way I work, the techniques I use, really vary from project to project.

AR: Can you summarize your design aesthetic in a sentence or two?

MC: It's the freedom from the obsession of form, from aesthetic conditioning, from any overly prescriptive style. Form and matter are elements of great expressiveness. Good design is both original and personal.

AR: How do you keep your environmental footprint to a minimum?

MC: Respect for the environment is part of our contemporary culture. It is a responsibility, both to ourselves and our children. I am by no means an environmental extremist, but it is of vital importance when working to think about the health of the en-

vironment and our own personal impact on it. All of my products are designed and manufactured in a way that keeps my environmental footprint to a minimum. How? Well, I might treat wood with oil, rather than varnish, for example.

AR: What are your favourite pieces you've designed in the Avenue Road collection?

MC: There are several Henge products in the Avenue Road collection, including my Pipe light range, my signature ringed lighting fixtures and items of furniture such as the Nomad coffee table, which is made from steel and stone. I find it difficult to choose my favourite piece, but these are some of the products to which I have a particular emotional attachment, and of which I feel most proud.

AR: What's the most important thing you have learned over the course of your career?

MC: To be humble, to be curious and to constantly question myself and my ideas.

Deborah Moss jokes that her end of Toronto's up-and-coming Junction neighbourhood will never be cool. "They stop the planters a block west of here," she says about a part of the city that until recently was better known for its pay-by-the-hour rooms than for the design studios and espresso bars that have since set up shop on the strip. But Moss, whose studio has been here for over eight years, shrugs and says, "If you move to the Junction, you deal with the history of the Junction."

Moss & Lam is a collaboration Moss started in 1989 with her late husband, Edward Lam. The studio is split into two entities. "The Collection is the child that we really love and want to grow," she says, "and Moss & Lam is a big grown-up that has a mind of its own sometimes." Their murals and interior installations can be found gracing grand hotels, restaurants and gleaming department stores the world over. The Collection is a series of furniture and art, taking the large-scale thinking of Moss & Lam's commercial projects and distilling it into something more palatable for everyday living spaces. Their fiercely

Facing page – There are no bare surfaces at the Moss & Lam studio, the place is stacked with paints, material simples, tools and odds and ends.

This page – Deborah Moss in her studio. The background is an unfinished canvas for a retail project in Shanghai.

A – SPREADS
The four "Influencer" features sit on different colour palettes. Each explores the life and works of key figures in the design industry. Reportage features include behind-the-scenes studio visits with local designers Moss & Lam.

NEXT PAGE – SPREADS
A home visit with interior designer Yabu Pushelberg

Nymphenburg Porcelain

A Fine Balance

Time stands still at the Nymphenburg Porcelain Manufactory in Munich. The workshop has remained in the same location for over 250 years, on the grounds of the Nymphenburg Palace. The benchmark baroque palace, which formerly housed the summering royal Bavarian family, now mostly bustles with camera-clutching tourists. Inside, each piece is still painstakingly crafted by hand; special orders can take up to two years to be completed. Electricity is strictly verboten – everything is water-powered by the stream running through the palace grounds, part of an adamant refusal to allow modern technology to disrupt the studio's established manufacturing traditions. Even the tiniest details are painted by hand, a skill that artisans perfect for up to 15 years, resulting in impeccable precision and impossibly expressive porcelain faces.

The workshop at the Nymphenburg Palace grounds

Nymphenburg was founded in 1747 under the Bavarian Elector Max III as a royal ceramics studio. At that time, Europe was enchanted by the baroque aesthetic, immortalized through doughy cherubs and ornamental flourishes. Porcelain was a favoured medium, having been directly imported from China since the Middle Ages, while European craftsmen were still figuring out how to produce the material.

The Wittelsbach coat of arms marks each piece

It took seven years of failed attempts after its foundation for Nymphenburg to perfect its own technique of mixing porcelain, a recipe that would still be used 250 years later.

Clara the rhinoceros, 1770

But while courtly figurines and hand-painted details may no longer be as *de rigueur* as they were in the 18th century, Nymphenburg has kept up with modern design language. Take Clara the rhinoceros, for example, a piece that dates back to the late 18th century, when people were fascinated with curiosities from afar. With textured skin covered in bumps and a somewhat glazed look in her eye (much like a porcelain rhinoceros would have), Clara has since been updated with a smart matte finish, and has even received a special-edition makeover by Karl Lagerfeld.

Bowl with hippopotamus by Hella Jongerius, 2004

Egg vase by Ted Muehling, 2000

The elegant egg vases by Ted Muehling, which come in a set of earthy hues, are a far cry from the factory's rococo roots. Collaborations with contemporary artists and designers, including Hella Jongerius and Konstantin Grcic, provide a compelling source of juxtapositions between centuries-old techniques and today's preferences. The studio has thus embraced a delicate balance between old and new, which, as 250 successful years can attest, will continue to evolve while honouring tradition.

64

"We haven't had our Hamptons house for long, but we're already in love with our Kimono sofa from Avenue Road. We chose it because we wanted the ultimate relaxation sofa that would seat at least eight people – it's so simple in aesthetic yet generous in size. The house is filled with things we collected and love, so the sofa is accessorized with West African native indigo pillows. It really is the most comfortable piece in the room; you just sink into it and take in the gorgeous view out to the ocean. No one ever wants to leave the comfort of this sofa."

Facing page – George and Glenn with their Kimono sofa

Above – Custom Lens table and benches by Marlieke Van Rossum

65

George Yabu and Glenn Pushelberg
Interior designers
The Hamptons

Clarity and simplicity give the bigger picture to an
array of projects, from fashion labels to law firms,
airlines to private banks.

Projects
USM Holdings | Nachmann Rechtsanwälte
Banque Heritage | Style Magazine
Swiss International Air Lines | Ionic Holdings

Client
USM Holdings

Country
Russia

Work
**Identity
Publishing
Digital design**

The brief for Russia's USM Holdings was to create an identity that highlighted the international reach of the brand and communicated the diversity of its portfolio. With USM's interests in steel and mining, telecoms, the Internet and media, it was important that the symbol and logotype should reflect this breadth.

In response, Winkreative crafted a minimalist, confidently spaced logotype that communicates the company's dynamic nature. Supported by a positive symbol that aligns with the progressive nature of USM, the overall look and feel of the identity is one of solidity and ambition.

A – IDENTITY
The identity for USM embodies fortitude, dynamism and growth, communicating the diversity of USM's portfolio.

A

B

B – COVER
The cover represents the
confidence of the brand,
wrapped with a screen-
printed bellyband.

C – SPREADS
The photography recalls
USM's Russian roots and
conveys the scale of the
company's operations.

C

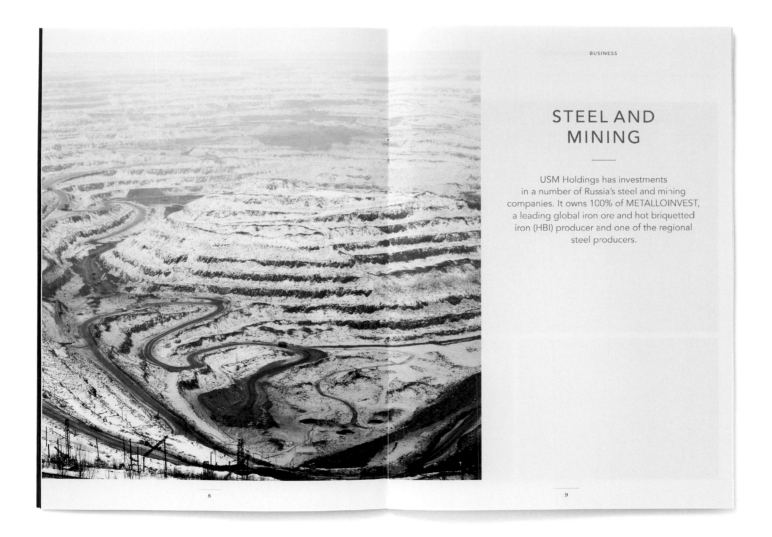

BUSINESS

STEEL AND MINING

USM Holdings has investments
in a number of Russia's steel and mining
companies. It owns 100% of METALLOINVEST,
a leading global iron ore and hot briquetted
iron (HBI) producer and one of the regional
steel producers.

8

9

Client
Nachmann Rechtsanwälte

Country
Germany

Work
**Identity
Advertising**

The Nachmann law firm needed a new identity to coincide with the opening of its head office in Munich. Winkreative's solution is clean and timeless, communicating the prestige needed to stand out in the legal trade while acknowledging the firm's Bavarian connection.

The identity encompasses a variety of applications, including Nachmann's website, stationery and office signage. Winkreative also used its interior design skills to build a branded office environment.

A

A – LOGO
A distinctive logotype and symbol together express an established law firm with a unique perspective.

OPPOSITE, NEXT PAGE –
ADVERTISING
An organised arrangement of all law firm office essentials includes additional character thanks to an elephant and a Rubik's Cube.

N Nachmann
Rechtsanwälte

Sind Ihre Füße zu groß, um in die Fußstapfen anderer zu treten?

... dann könnte dieser Platz schon bald der Ihre sein.

Exzellenz. Innovationskraft. Kreativität. Menschlichkeit. Bodenhaftung. Konzentration auf das, was unsere Mandanten wirklich weiter bringt. Wenn Sie diese Werte als Herausforderung betrachten, dann sollten wir uns kennenlernen. Denn zur Verstärkung unseres engagierten Teams suchen wir:

Rechtsanwalt Baurecht (m/w)

Sie verfügen über fundierte Berufserfahrung im privaten Baurecht, Knowhow in der Abwicklung von M&A-Projekten und Beratungskompetenz bei Immobilienfinanzierungen? Dann informieren Sie sich jetzt unter:

www.nachmann.com/jobs

nachmann.com

Nachmann
Insolvenzverwaltung

Das Einfache war
Ihnen schon immer viel
zu leicht?

... dann könnte dieser Platz schon bald
der Ihre sein.

Exzellenz. Innovationskraft. Kreativität.
Menschlichkeit. Bodenhaftung. Konzentration auf das, was unsere Mandanten
wirklich weiter bringt. Wenn Sie diese
Werte als Herausforderung betrachten,
dann sollten wir uns kennenlernen.
Denn zur Verstärkung unseres engagierten Teams suchen wir:

Rechtsanwalt
Insolvenzrecht (m/w)

Sie verfügen über mindestens 3 Jahre
Berufserfahrung im Bereich Insolvenzrecht
und ein ausgeprägtes Verständnis für
wirtschaftliche Zusammenhänge?
Dann informieren Sie sich jetzt unter:

www.nachmann.com/jobs

nachmann.com

Client
Banque Heritage

Country
Switzerland

Work
**Identity
Publishing
Digital design**

Banque Heritage is a private Swiss bank based in Geneva. The family business specialises in asset management for private clients and institutional investors. Its 20th anniversary, in 2006, was the perfect opportunity for Winkreative to develop a new identity and website and new printed collateral for the bank.

Banque Heritage's interest in the arts and sciences was a key point of inspiration. A contemporary typeface was combined with a warm colour palette for a sophisticated identity that reflects not only the provenance but also the modernity of the bank.

A

⊞ BANQUE HERITAGE

A – DENTITY
The composite H logo conveys solidity and the bank's Swiss heritage and is complemented by a modern typeface.

NEXT PAGE –
PHOTOGRAPHY
Winkreative commissioned and art-directed photography to give added impact to the bank's printed materials.

Banque Heritage **Clarity**

Client
Style Magazine

Country
Italy

Work
Publishing

Style Magazine, a supplement to one of Italy's oldest and most respected newspapers, *Corriere della Sera*, has a contemporary incarnation thanks to an intensive Wink-eative redesign.

In addition to an intelligent new design and layout, there's a fresh editorial approach, including six unique sections covering everything from street style to business ethics.

A

A – COVER
Winkreative designed a bespoke masthead and typeface system, and introduced a new photographic direction, recommending photographers and stylists.

DI MARIA LUISA BONACCHI

FOTO DI GUIDO FUÀ PER STYLE

Savile vicolo

È la risposta alla londinesissima Savile Row. Ma è nata un bel pezzo prima. Tra le stradine, i viali, i capolavori anneriti del Settecento, in mezzo al profumo di caffè, ci sono le botteghe della vera eleganza. Artigiani e artisti. Del taglio d'abito, della scarpa, della cravatta, del guanto e dell'ombrello. Ecco la guida di Style

Renato Ciardi, 77 anni e un gusto perfetto. Lui dice che «la sartoria a Napoli è cosa delicata e meticolosa».

A COPENHAGEN GLI SPAZZOLINI SONO BIODEGRADABILI E LA SPAZZATURA DIVENTA BIOGAS. UN MODELLO IMITATO OVUNQUE, DAI CUCUZZOLI AL DESERTO

Darsi una mano di: verde non basta: nelle nuove mete del lusso l'hammam funziona a riciclo di biomasse e il croissant si cuoce sui sassi. L'hotel premiato da l'Ecotourism Award come il più verde al mondo è il lussuoso Crowne Plaza di Copenhagen (www.cpcopenhagen.dk): la facciata «ospita» un grande parco di pannelli solari, la gestione dei consumi è computerizzata, gli spazzolini da denti sono biodegradabili, i rifiuti vengono trasformati in biogas. Un modello imitato ovunque, anche tra monti, deserti e lagune, per andare incontro a tutti i viaggiatori che, per dirla con il Guardian, «mettono in valigia con il costume da bagno anche il cervello».

Eremi e palazzi: eco, spesso certificati, che hanno fatto dell'accoppiata sostenibilità-charme una bandiera. Qualche esempio? Il camp high-tech Whitepod, 30 tende geodetiche ai piedi del lato elvetico de Dent du Midi (www.whitepod.com); l'Hotel Saratz di Pontresina, Engadina, che si è riconvertito al 90 per cento all'uso del riscaldamento geotermico (www.saratz. ch); le 13 stanze, ricostruite con materiali naturali sulle fondamenta medievali, nel bosco di Vlatos, a Creta (www.milia.gr); i bed and breakfast Domus Amigas in Sardegna, dove si tiene perfino un corso per fabbricare bio-mattoni (www.domusamigas.it); l'Antico Casale di Montegualandro & Spa, in provincia di Perugia, unica struttura umbra con certificazione ambientale Ecola-

FTO: ZEFA/CORBIS/SIE • TIMOTHEA AMBROSETTI

bel (www.anticocasale.it). Anche l'Africa si è adeguata: al Bulungula Lodge di Mthatha (www.bulungula.com), in Sudafrica, il pane è cotto sulla roccia, mentre il Safari Lodge San Camp, in Botswana (www.ecoluxury.com), si alimenta esclusivamente con energia solare.

Tornando in Italia, l'Alto Adige è una regione-modello per la bioarchitettura, dove anche gli hotel devono essere per legge a prova di benessere, dentro e fuori. Da primato il Theiner's Garten Bio Vitalhotel di Gargazzone (Bz): nel centro della distesa di frutteti più grande d'Europa, è realizzato in pino cembro (abbattuto durante la fase lunare propizia). Ospita un'azienda biologica e una zona benessere dove i trattamenti si basano sulle teorie olistiche di Sebastian Kneipp, e poi il giardino dei sensi dove farsi massaggiare fra gli alberi, la palestra sul tetto, l'orto che offre frutta e cucina bio… Su ogni terrazzo c'è una pergola con la vite, nelle camere nessun dispositivo elettrico per non disturbare il sonno: i letti sono privi di parti in metallo e i materassi al 100 per cento naturali. Ovviamente, anche le escursioni sono all'insegna del benessere eco, gite sui sentieri lungo i vecchi canali con Walter Theiner, «biobicitour» e lezioni di nordic walking.

Tutta un'altra storia, quella raccontata dai proprietari della Masseria Salamina in Puglia: quando hanno incominciato a scavare tra ulivi secolari e fondamenta del Quattrocento per realizzare i tubi del teleriscaldamento ci

Nelle pagine in apertura: il Safari Lodge San Camp nel Parco Makgadikgadi Pans, in Botswana, si alimenta esclusivamente con energia solare.

Una reggia nel deserto: è il Feynan Lodge, in Giordania. Sotto: l'altoatesino Theiner's Garten Bio Vitalhotel, con orto bio (a destra). Nella pagina accanto, il Nuovo Rifugio Monte Rosa, in Svizzera: incastrato fra i ghiacci, a 2.883 metri, produce il 90 per cento dell'energia di cui necessita.

davano per matti, ora i loro sforzi sono stati riconosciuti dal premio Oscar Green. La chiara villa merlata conserva il fascino della storica casa di campagna dei Salamina (si chiamava così già nel Seicento), con le frivoli torri ottocentesche, la cappella settecentesca, le volte dei vecchi frantoi, i mobili dall'eleganza classica, le camere bianche nell'ex ovile. Ma il passato convive con la modernità: impianti a basso consumo, vasche idromassaggio e wi-fi. Tra gli ospiti c'è chi si accontenta della tranquillità del patio e della piscina a sfioro, con mosaici di vetro e acqua salata. E chi, invece, preferisce potare, sarchiare e fare provviste di verdure, marmellate e creme di bellezza all'olio; oppure visitare l'oasi Wwf di Torre Guaceto, prendere il sole sulla spiaggia di Torre Canne, cercare conchiglie fossili al Parco delle Dune.

Se proprio bisogna scegliere, l'eco-costruzione più stupefacente è in Svizzera: il Nuovo Rifugio Monte Rosa, piantato avveniristicamente nella roccia i seracchi del ghiacciaio Gornergrat, non a caso vincitore del premio Milestone per lo sviluppo sostenibile e insignito del Premio Solare 2010 nella categoria nuove costruzioni. Per far passare agli alpinisti provetti una notte con tutte le comodità a 2.883 metri, gli architetti del Politecnico di Zurigo si sono cimentati in una prova quasi impossibile: trasformare la storica Capanna Monte Rosa, se non in un resort, di certo nel nido d'aquila più comodo del mondo. Il nuovo rifugio ha pareti di acciaio, legno e cristallo, le camere e

A

HOMO ELEGANS

100 ANNI
DA YANEZ

Sentirsi avventurieri e corsari, nel segno del basic vissuto. Ma senza abbandonare la giungla metropolitana. Fatevi guidare da queste pagine. E da un libro appena uscito (Neri Pozza): *La tempestosa vita di capitan Salgari* di Silvano Gonzato. A un secolo dalla scomparsa ispirarsi allo scrittore di Sandokan e ai suoi eroi

DI ALESSANDRO CALASCIBETTA
FOTO DI MICHAEL WOOLLEY

L'ACCESSORIO NON FA UNA SMORFIA

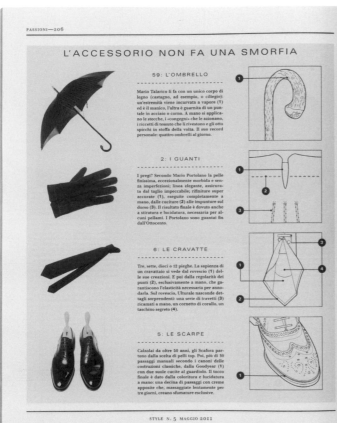

59: L'OMBRELLO

Mario Talarico li fa con un unico corpo di legno (castagna, ad esempio, o ciliegio): un'estremità viene incurvata a vapore (1) ed è il manico, l'altra è guarnita di un puntale in acciaio o corno. A mano si applicano le stecche, i «congegni» che le azionano, i riccetti di tessuto che li rivestono e gli otto spicchi in stoffa della volta. Il suo record personale: quattro ombrelli al giorno.

2: I GUANTI

I pregi? Secondo Mario Portolano la pelle finissima, eccezionalmente morbida e senza imperfezioni; linea elegante, assicurata dal taglio impeccabile; rifiniture super accurate (1), eseguite completamente a mano, dalle cuciture (2) alle impunture sul dorso (3). Il risultato finale è dovuto anche a stiratura e lucidatura, necessaria per alcuni pellami. I Portolano sono guantai fin dall'Ottocento.

6: LE CRAVATTE

Tre, sette, dieci o 12 pieghe. La sapienza di un cravattaio si vede dal rovescio (1) delle sue creazioni. E poi dalla regolarità dei punti (2), esclusivamente a mano, che garantiscono l'elasticità necessaria per annodarla. Sul rovescio, Ulturale nasconde dettagli sorprendenti: una serie di travetti (3) ricamati a mano, un cornetto di corallo, un taschino segreto (4).

5: LE SCARPE

Calzolai da oltre 50 anni, gli Scafora partono dalla scelta dei pelli top. Poi, più di 30 passaggi manuali secondo i canoni delle costruzioni classiche, dalla Goodyear (1) con due suole cucite al guardiolo. Il tocco finale è dato dalla coloritura e lucidatura a mano: una decina di passaggi con creme apposite che, massaggiate lentamente per tre giorni, creano sfumature esclusive.

DA QUI IN AMERICA

Mario Talarico è quasi un'icona; fa ombrelli, richiesti nel mondo, da quando aveva 12 anni. Oggi ne ha 79.

QUASI UNO AL GIORNO (FERIALE)

Nella sartoria di Gennaro Solito, in un palazzo antico, si confezionano una ventina di abiti in un mese.

VICINI SENZA «FARSI LE SCARPE»

Le cravatte di Ulturale in mostra nella boutique di via Carlo Poerio. Non lontano da quella di Maurizio Marinella.

DALLA TESTA AI PIEDI

Nell'emporio della famiglia Cilento si trova il miglior artigianato maschile. Le scarpe sono passione pura.

In sartoria ci si va anche per bere un caffè

E se camiciai made in Napoli sono senza dubbio Luigi e Fabio Borrelli, si fanno strada anche giovani come Luca Avitabile di Satriano Cinque (dal nome del vicolo): «La camicia è una seconda pelle; perché sia perfetta ci vuole una tecnica di base che si affina con l'esperienza del fatto a mano, dall'inizio alla fine». È la regola che vale per tutti gli accessori dell'eleganza, i campani lo sanno bene. Come la scarpa artigianale con lavorazione Goodyear eseguita alla perfezione, meglio dei maestri calzolai della contea inglese di Northampton. Due nomi dall'ultima generazione? Paolo Scafora (pelli pregiate e comfort imbattibile) e Vito Viscido (stupendi i mocassini marchio Castori di pelle scamosciata «cashmere»). Senza dimenticare i guanti, che nei Settecento-Ottocento erano il vanto di Napoli capitale, concentrati nel rione Sanità. Ricerca accurata delle pelli, di cui ri-

noscere imperfezioni e venature, taglio preciso, cuciture e impunture eseguite con finezza e precisione sono l'eredità di Mario Portolano, guantaio celeberrimo. Quasi quanto lo è il re degli ombrelli, il mitico Mario Talarico, 79 anni. Lo trovate con il nipote Mario junior ai bordi dei quartieri spagnoli: cercate l'ombrellino colorato legato a un terrazzino con più giri di nastro adesivo. Sotto, in un antro zeppo di parapioggia fra cui occhieggiano Padre Pio, il cornetto di corallo e una manina grattaschiena, c'è lui: «Da 67 anni sto seduto a chillo deschetto della bisnonna» dice mostrando lo Spillo, l'ombrello in seta e bambù, dalle proporzioni perfette, identico a quello usato da lord Chamberlain. «Io gli ombrelli di Talarico li porto a passeggio» conclude Massaccesi, «ma non li lascio mai. Perché fidarsi è bene, ma questi, se incustoditi, non li ritrovate più».

The magazine cover reads:

CORRIERE DELLA SERA

STYLE MAGAZINE

ECONOMIA & ETICA
Aziende controcorrente:
Luxottica. Un piano per
la felicità. Lo racconta
l'a.d. Andrea Guerra.

INDISCRETO
Casini scatenato, parla
di pubblico e privato.
Dalla moglie al
«Berlusconi fallito».

IMPOSSIBILE
Albertina Carraro.
Bellissima, trasgressiva.
Ha un fidanzato col
doppio dei suoi anni.

INTERNI
La casa fattoria di
Zucchero: si fa musica
tra galline, troni, trote
e un autobus in salotto.

MENSILE DEL CORRIERE DELLA SERA — MAGGIO 2011

**PREVIOUS PAGE, A –
SPREADS**
Bold lines, graphic
elements, symbols
and illustration enable
easier navigation
and readability.

Swiss International Air Lines

Country
Switzerland

Work
Strategy
Identity
Publishing
Digital design
Environment

For the relaunch of Switzerland's national airline, Winkreative devised a clear brand architecture to construct a new identity for the renamed carrier, reinvigorating every area of the business. Design work included naming, corporate identity, aircraft liveries, ground and in-flight passenger items, corporate signage, website and advertising.

The corporate identity is a direct reference to the country's heritage: a clean and understated reflection of Swiss graphic design. After developing detailed design specifications, Winkreative assigned a leading architect to remodel the Swiss airport lounge and ticket-office interiors. The aircraft cabin interiors were also redesigned, with bespoke fabrics and materials.

A – IDENTITY
Winkreative simplified
the full name of the
airline to SWISS and
incorporated the cross
symbol of Switzerland.
The cube device was
inspired by the perfectly
square dimensions of
the Swiss flag.

B – TYPOGRAPHY
The CH Sans custom
typeface, which is
rooted in Swiss sans serif
heritage, was specially
commissioned.

C – COLOUR PALETTE
The palette of white and
earthy tones was inspired
by the Swiss landscape.

B

Bietschhorn 3934m
Airbus A320–214

Pizol 2844m
Airbus A320–214

Les Diablerets 3210m
Airbus A320–214

Swiss International Air Lines
Typography

CH Sans Regular
abcdefghijklmnop qrstuvwxyz
ABCDEFGHIJKLMNOPQRSTUVWXYZ
0123456789 €$%&(.,;:#!?)

CH Sans Bold
abcdefghijklmnopqrstuvwxyz
ABCDEFGHIJKLMNOPQRSTUVWXYZ
0123456789 €$%&(.,;:#!?)

C

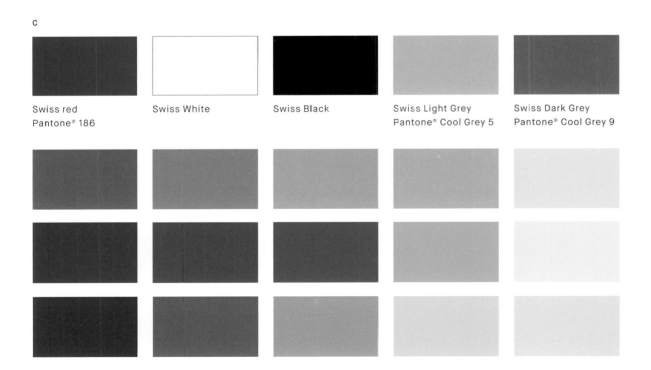

Swiss red
Pantone® 186

Swiss White

Swiss Black

Swiss Light Grey
Pantone® Cool Grey 5

Swiss Dark Grey
Pantone® Cool Grey 9

A, C – LIVERY
To convey a sense of national identity, the four national languages of Switzerland are listed next to the name on each aircraft in the fleet.

B – SIGNAGE
The red cube device is used at key points of service.

A

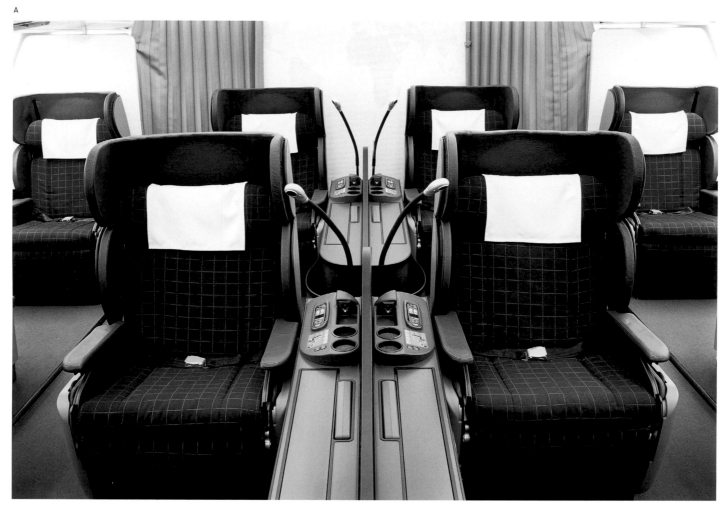

B

A – INTERIORS
Winkreative
commissioned a textile
designer to create
bespoke seat fabrics and
specified interior details.

B – PRINTED MATERIALS
Winkreative designed
all the printed materials,
from aircraft safety
cards to the company's
annual report.

C – PRINTED MATERIAL
The SWISS commercial
fleet for winter 2003–4
used in the annual
report.

C

AIRBUS A340

BOEING MD-11[2]

AIRBUS A330

AIRBUS A321

AIRBUS A320

AIRBUS A319

AVRO RJ-100

AVRO RJ-85

EMBRAER 145

SAAB 2000

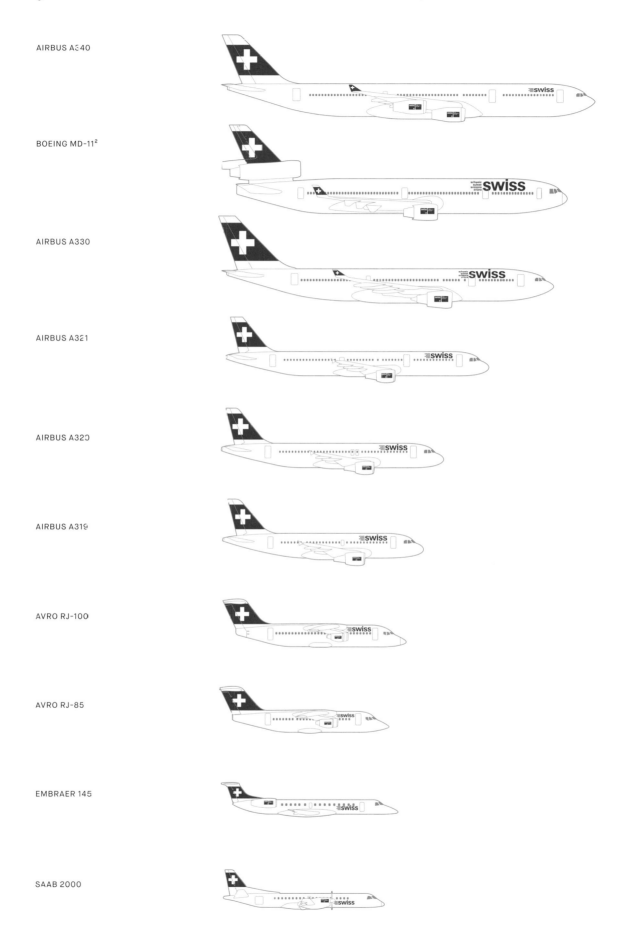

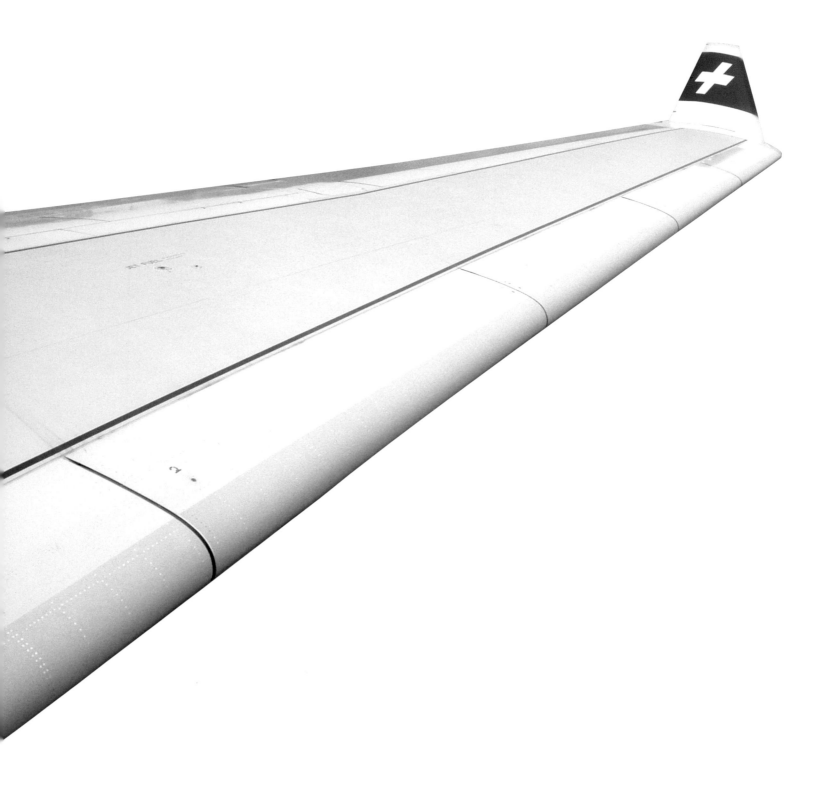

A – PHOTOGRAPHY
Launch aircraft imagery
by Christopher Griffith.

B – PRINTED MATERIAL
The brand guidelines
book was almost 600
pages long.

B

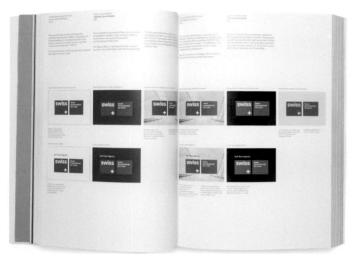

A – BRAND BOOK
Two brand books were produced in support of the launch to communicate the new vision of the brand.

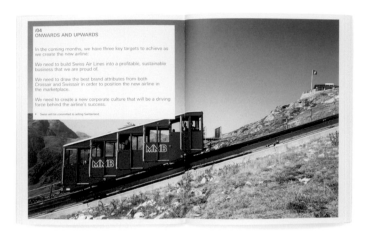

/07
OUR SWISSNESS

The new airline has a powerful brand heritage that will propel it forward. The past success and status of the brand stem from its Swiss origin and it is this dedication to 'Swissness' that will define the future.

There are a number of values common to both Swissair and Crossair which mirror the values of Switzerland: quality, prestige, tradition in care, service, efficiency, security, reliability, cleanliness and Swiss heritage.

Universally accepted and well-respected, these Swiss values will be coveted by consumers looking for a superior travel experience.

/11
CONCLUSION

Through innovations in everything from route strategies to in-flight service to marketing alliances, Swiss is an airline that will define a whole new market segment and establish itself as the new benchmark at the top end of the industry. By building on Switzerland's exceptional infrastructure, developing its hubs and offering passengers a product that will immediately translate into loyalty, Swiss is destined to evolve into one of the world's most respected and iconic brands.

Client
Ionic Holdings
Country
Greece
Work
Identity

When Ionic Holdings approached Winkreative to design a brand identity for its new shipping company, we seized the opportunity to take to the high seas.

The handcrafted logotype is solid yet dynamic, expressing strength and industry, while the marque, based on a flag in motion, imparts a sense of fluidity and vigour to the identity.

Because the logotype was designed to work on hugely varied scales – from business cards to cargo ships – legibility was key.

The resulting identity successfully portrays the company as a progressive global venture, with a subtle nod to its Greek heritage thanks to a colour palette that includes crisp nautical white and Ionian blue.

A

A – LOGO
The stencilled graphic lettering plays with shipping-container vernacular, while the blue in the flag recognises Ionic's Greek heritage.

NEXT PAGE – CARGO SHIP
The boldness of the logo mirrors the heavyweight girders on board.

Craft

Just as Lexus demonstrates unbridled craftsmanship in its quest for new luxury, so we also continue to expand our manual to execute work that is fit for purpose for the brands we serve. Building strong, relevant foundations, to which a brand always stays true, is as it should be. Our craft is going further and diving into the details – the different materials, styles, techniques and processes that can be used to convey something unique. Collaboration with others – from singularly expert Japanese artisans for Lexus and luxury international makers for BlackBerry, to locally based photographers and writers for the truly Brazilian *Wish Casa* – gives us a vast pool of resources with which we can cover every detail of a coherent, authentic and sometimes unconventional brand experience. Design can now be delivered in ways previously unimaginable, but the tools of our craft – intuition, ideas and growing global resources – remain constant.

The Craft Business

Using a strategy anchored in narrative, Winkreative works
with the brand values of Lexus to develop a fresh and
relevant voice in the design world. Atsushi Takada, general
manager of Lexus International, describes the process.

In addition to developing pioneering hybrid technology through a characteristically Japanese approach to design and craftsmanship, Lexus strives to examine the wider territory of intelligent design. By connecting with its customers in exciting new ways, the brand looks to the future and goes beyond the expected.

Winkreative
What single thing has most transformed the motor industry in the past decade?

Takada-san
Environmental issues. There are two aspects to this – the tightening up of the regulations for CO_2 emissions in the world, and the tendency for customers to lean towards more environmentally friendly products. Sales of hybrid cars, which are economical as well as environmental, show that the customer mindset has definitely changed.

Winkreative
What makes Lexus distinctly Japanese?

Takada-san
We never intended to push the brand as something distinctly Japanese, but I think it has become one as a result. I think the three aspects that make Lexus distinctly Japanese are environmental awareness, craftsmanship and hospitality. We have a term, *mottainai*, which conveys a sense of regret concerning waste. Japanese people have always had respect for the environment. Craftsmanship and hospitality are a part of the Japanese sensibility and have become the strength of the brand; as a result, they have made Lexus distinctly Japanese.

Winkreative
Could you explain the notion of *takumi*?

Takada-san
I think the English word for *takumi* would be craftsmanship. There are two different kinds of people making things. One is artists and designers, people who create things under an artistic vision. In our company, the car designers would fit in the artists category. On the other hand, *takumi* is someone who creates things using high-level specialist skills. At Lexus, we respect craftsmen who produce elaborate work in exactly the same way as we respect designers and artists.

Winkreative
What are your thoughts on technology and its influence on craft?

Takada-san
I'm not sure how to answer this. I think there are two kinds of technology: the first one is the kind that changes how society exists or changes the fundamental aspect of cars. For example, hybrid engines and hydrogen engines, which will be introduced in the future, and electric cars – these will change industry and society fundamentally. The second type of technology is about improving what is currently used in cars. I think all car companies are endeavouring to innovate and improve the technology, and among those companies, I'm confident that Lexus will win over the others. The Lexus ideology is to keep improving day by day.

Winkreative
Hybrid technology is a core benefit of the Lexus brand – when did these conversations start? What was the impetus?

Takada-san
Hybrid technology is something that's valued by the Toyota Corporation as a whole. I'm not sure exactly when we started the discussion, but in the early 90s we launched a project to make an innovative car in the run-up to the 21st century. We had numerous trials and errors, and finally, in 1997, we had our first hybrid car, the Toyota Prius. Lexus is a result of our continuous endeavour to make a hybrid car, building on experiences and assets we have developed over the years.

Winkreative
How important is good design? Would you say that good design is often unseen design?

Takada-san
Some of the most important factors for a car are its motion and travel performance, its functionality and inside space. However, in the end, customers always make a choice based on the design, which has been proven by extensive research. There are lots of definitions of design. Good design isn't always immediately obvious, but at the same time it isn't always unseen. What we've always tried to do with Lexus is excite the customer and lift their spirits. If you look at other cars like Ferrari and Lamborghini, they all have a really distinct design, which creates a strong character that is easy to recognise. A sedan is very small and cute, and conveys this message to customers through the design, which is really important. I think that all cars, especially luxury cars, should clearly express their message through their design.

Winkreative
Why is the championing of emerging design talent so important to Lexus?

Takada-san
Sustainability is the main reason. By supporting younger generations and encouraging them to succeed, we are creating a sustainable society and economy.

Winkreative
Why do you think you are in our "Craft" chapter?

Takada-san
Well, if Lexus was selected for this chapter because of its craftsmanship and artisanship, then I suppose it's because we're understood as a brand that uses really skilled craft to make beautiful high-end products, which in the end become something very luxurious. Winkreative understands that this is what we're trying to do; it's not just about the surface.

Winkreative
What does the future of Lexus production hold?

Takada-san
What we'd like to do in the future is to establish a new category for luxury brands. As we've come into the 21st century, there's a lot more interest in environmental issues, as well as new types of affluent people emerging all over the world. I think that, because of these things, the definition of luxury brands, including fashion brands, will change. We'd like Lexus to represent a new type of luxury car brand.

Winkreative
What were you looking for from Winkreative?

Takada-san
Winkreative has very up-to-date information, which is global and wide-ranging and something that few of us in the car industry have. We have really benefited from being given new concepts and ideas based on this information.

Winkreative
How has the work changed the business? What does the Winkreative aesthetic lend to your business?

Takada-san
I feel that everyone at Winkreative, led by Tyler's ideology, has great information and knowledge of design, culture and aesthetics. We wanted to create a new definition of luxury, and it is something we wouldn't have been able to do without Winkreative's help and backup, so we're grateful for all the ideas that they've shared with us. Winkreative's vision is going to lead the luxury industry into becoming something new and exciting – it is a vision for the future.

By supporting younger generations and encouraging them to succeed, we are creating a sustainable society and economy.

Winkreative
A well-designed car should be...

Takada-san
That's a really difficult question. It's about industrial design, so it has to function well, but in addition to that you need to create luxuriousness. A well-functioning car is not enough any more, so we need to create a really nice design that enriches people's minds just by looking at it. A well-designed car should inspire people.

Lexus International

Country
Japan
Work
Strategy
Publishing
Identity
Environment
Film

Winkreative's work with Lexus is part of a long-term assignment as external brand advisers. To enhance the brands image globally, we dived into more than two decades of history to identify its strengths and help articulate its stories more effectively. As a leader in the luxury hybrid car market, Lexus has a natural and authentic alignment with great design. Using craft and innovation as a platform and employing a narrative-based approach, Winkreative carved out the rich new territory of design and environment, giving Lexus the opportunity to explore all fields of design in an authentic way. Out of this came four distinct projects – *Beyond* magazine, the Lexus Design Award, Crafted and Intersect, all of which reinforce Lexus's commitment to craftsmanship, respect for nature and the pursuit of perfection in design.

Beyond **magazine** – The international biannual magazine *Beyond* marks a bold direction for the Lexus brand. Following Winkreative's strategic review, Lexus ventured into rich new territory, exploring how craftsmanship, respect for nature and the pursuit of perfection in design drive the brand. With 500,000 global readers, *Beyond* includes interviews with design luminaries, profiles of the master craftspeople who work with Lexus and in-depth reports on product design.

A

A – COVER
The name *Beyond* refers to Lexus's venturing beyond the expected and into new territories. The composite cover differentiates *Beyond* from other car magazines, alluding to design and lifestyle as well as cars.

A

BEYOND

BY LEXUS

A JOURNAL ON DESIGN AND CRAFTSMANSHIP

B

 1 5  10 20

A – IDENTITY
Working with the classic Dutch sans serif typeface Nobel, the masthead presents the established brand with a new perspective.

B – NUMBERING DEVICES
The design of the accelerating chapter numbers is drawn from geometric shapes, reflecting the movement of cars on roads.

C – CONTENTS PAGE
Cropped images provide a preview of upcoming content.

D – TITLE PAGES
The numerals 1, 5, 10 and 20 loosely reference car acceleration and provide visual breaks throughout the magazine.

C

BEYOND BY LEXUS

CONTENTS

CONTENTS 5

Vehicle specifications are correct at the time of going to press. The car models shown may not be available in all countries. Please contact your local Lexus dealership for more information.

THE GALLERY'S
A STAGE, AND
THE AUDIENCE
CAN COME
ONSTAGE AND
PARTICIPATE

Bold pull-quotes
and technical specs
interspersed throughout
the design help frame the
photography.

B, C – SPREADS
A moment of surprise:
the best shots deserve
more exposure.
Immersive full-bleed
spreads and gatefolds
help readers experience
the complete journey.

THE LAB

TRACK
RECORD

WE TAKE A LEXUS LFA FOR A TURN AT SHIBETSU, THE VAST
PROVING GROUND IN NORTHERN JAPAN, WHERE SOME 200 TEST-DRIVERS
PUT THE LATEST MODELS THROUGH THEIR PACES EVERY DAY

TEXT BY SHOGO HAGIWARA AND PHOTOGRAPHY BY KOHEI TAKE

C

ONE COMES
ACROSS
THE MOST
SURPRISING
THINGS WHEN
ONE IS JUST
DRIFTING
AROUND THE
LANDSCAPE

D – SPREADS
Varied layouts,
photography and
illustration keep
the pace of the
magazine engaging.

NEXT PAGES –
PHOTOGRAPHY
Natural light accentuates
the shapes and contours
of the car while still
emphasising its key
features.

D

MAKING
AN ENTRANCE

THERE IS NO
MONEY THAT
COULD PAY FOR
THE EMOTION
I FEEL WHEN I
SEE A PROJECT
FINISHED

LEXUS
DESIGN
AWARD

The Lexus Design Award – Winkreative devised the Lexus Design Award, an international design competition initiated to firmly align Lexus with the world of design. Launched at Tokyo Designers Week 2012, the competition asked innovators from any design field for solutions to issues in everyday life relating to the theme of motion. Winkreative developed the logotype and environment concept, a series of print posters and a video with renowned product designer Sam Hecht.

A – LOGO
The logotype was drawn from a modified version of the Nobel typeface.

B – TYPEFACE
The bespoke typeface was designed as an exhibition font, reading clearly at a larger scale and across signage.

OPPOSITE – PATTERN
The pattern was inspired by the graphic horizontal lines of the exhibition space.

NEXT PAGES –
EXHIBITION SPACE
Based on the theme of motion, the hanging display walls of the installation were made with suspended paper tubes, creating a sense of movement and fluidity in the space.

Square Ballon 2007

ンヤメト

Junya Ishigami
Architect
Born in Kanagawa, Japan in 1974, he
graduated from Tokyo National
University of Fine Arts and Music with an
M.F.A in Architecture. His public works
include Kanagawa Institute of Technology
KAIT workshop (Atsugi), and yohji
yamamoto New York gansevoort street
store (New York). In 2005, he created
the furniture and also worked as special
designer for Lexus L-finesse Modern
Japanese Art Meets Automotive Design.
Awards include the BCS Prize in 2009,
the Golden Lion Award in part of the 12th
International Architecture Exhibition at
the Venice Biennale in 2010 and the
Commissioner for Cultural Affairs Award
in Japan in 2012. He is the author of
Another Scale of Architecture and other

1974年、神奈川県生まれ。2000年、
東京藝術大学大学院美術研究科
建築専攻修士課程修了。主な作品は
建築専攻修士課程修了。主な作品は
建築専攻大学KAIT工房（厚木市）、
（神奈川工科大学KAIT工房（厚木市）、
（yohji yamamoto store
gansevoort street store New York
（ニューヨーク）など。2005年には
Lexus L-finesse Modern Japanese
Art Meets Automotive Designの空間
構成、家具製作を担当。2009年度BCS
賞（建築業協会賞 特別賞）、2010年度
第12回ヴェネチア・ビエンナーレ国際
建築展 金獅子賞、2010年度毎日
デザイン賞、2012年度文化庁長官表彰
国際芸術部門賞他。受賞歴多数。
著書に『建築のあたらしい大きさ』など
がある。

Biennale Architecture Exhibition 2008 Japanese Pavilion

JUNYA

ISHIGAMI

yamamoto New York gansevoort street store 2008

Kanagawa Institute of technology KAIT workshop

Table 2005

INTERSECT
BY LEXUS

Intersect by Lexus – As Lexus continues to redefine luxury, Winkreative devised Intersect – a new form of brand experience. We collaborated with the prestigious architect and interior designer Wonderwall, transforming a glass cube in Tokyo's Aoyama fashion district into a luxury space. With a private lounge, an exhibition space, a carefully curated library and plenty of paraphernalia for discerning car buffs, Intersect communicates the brand's values in an innovative and engaging way.

OPPOSITE – PATTERN
Inspired by the iconic Lexus spindle grille, the pattern is designed to reflect key features of the shop interiors.

A – LOGO
The chiselled logotype is a gentle reminder of Lexus's investment in craft and design.

B – SHOP SPACE
Tokyo-based architect Wonderwall designed the interiors of the Intersect space, transforming a low-rise glass cube into a carefully curated brand experience, consolidating all that Lexus stands for under one roof.

B

CRAFTED
FOR LEXUS

Crafted for Lexus – Crafted is a collection of products by emerging Japanese artisans. Centred on three categories of - work, play and drive - Crafted for Lexus celebrates the craftsmanship of quality goods, spotlighting the artisans of tomorrow.

B

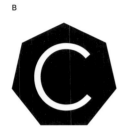

A – LOGO
The Crafted for Lexus logo is used across a range of products, from luggage to sunglasses.

B – SYMBOL
The symbol is designed to complement the logotype and can be used independently as a stamp for branding products.

C – PATTERN
The pattern is derived from the shape of the marque.

OPPOSITE – CAFÉ
The Intersect café.

C

A – CRAFTED FOR LEXUS
PRODUCTS
Clockwise from top
right: handcrafted
sunglasses by Kaneko
Optical; hand-sewn
leather iPhone cases and
iPad case by Rhythm;
waxed and waterproof,
Tembea's all-weather
canvas tote is built to
endure; the leather used
for Roberu's handmade
bags is steeped in
organic tannins and oil
to preserve its natural
character; for Ito's
stationery, the craft is
all in the touch; Tamaki
Niime's scarves are
woven using traditional
Japanese techniques.

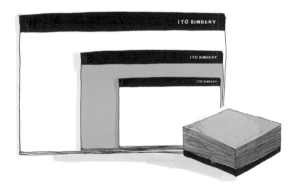

The Pleasure Principle

Brazil's strong culture of design celebrates the joy of living.

Look down at the streets of Brazil's capital city and you will see its design heritage gleaming beneath your feet. Black-and-white mosaics whirl down the pavements and across the avenues, saturating Rio de Janeiro's public spaces in lively pattern. A mark of its Portuguese heritage, the *calçada portuguesa* – mosaics of white limestone and black basalt – undulate in waves along three miles 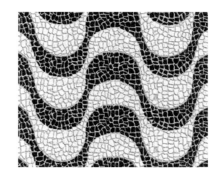 of Copacabana Beach, cover the sidewalks of São Paulo in stylised monochrome motifs and are said to continue to the Amazonian forest. Apart from the intervention of construction workers who have removed stones and put them back in random formations, these intricate works of art remain largely untouched and make up just a small part of Brazil's treasury of textures and heritage of dynamic design.

The textural journey continues from the floors, up the walls and across the façades of Brazil's civic and domestic architecture and has slowly produced a singular spirited style that is hard to mistake.

Rich woods, humble concrete, smooth marble, rough brick and native stone combine harmoniously against a healthy array of lush vegetation. But let's start with Oscar Niemeyer. Arguably a force behind Brazil's current creative culture, "the man who built Brasilia" changed the country's design destiny with his unapologetic, eye-catching civic monuments of the 1950s, when fluid swathes of smooth white marble began to emerge across the capital city. In a feat of political and design daring, Niemeyer single-handedly transformed architecture into a wonder of sensuous curves, lightness and unforgettable forms, adapting modern architecture to suit the context of Brazil. His "happily inventive" buildings connect with nature and invite the public to wholeheartedly embrace the pleasures of living.

Brazil's rich architectural ancestry has defined a creative identity, and today even the most functional Brazilian architecture is suffused with warmth and soul. Both a product and definer of Brazilian modernism, the muralist Paulo Werneck created a legacy that lives on in the flowing powdery-blue mosaics that adorn Brazil's buildings and walkways. Isay Weinfeld, one of the most renowned and sought-after architects working in Brazil today, suggests that Brazilian architecture "has no particular style", instead having a "patina that symbolises a richness of materiality". But perhaps it's this materiality that defines Brazilian style? Weinfeld's Fasano hotel is a great example: it's minimal and functional, but the materials – dark local rosewood, exposed brick, polished marble, sultry worn leather – exude sophistication and sensuality. The rational proportions and wide spaces nod to modernist templates, but this is minimalism the Latin way – in sexy overdrive, and the experience is pure pleasure.

Architects and designers adhere to global trends, but the tropicalism of the geography and tactility of natural materials create a distinct, organic style that echoes Brazil's dynamism. Meanwhile, on the streets, art movements such as *lambe-lambe* celebrate the raw, vibrant heart of the cities. *Lambe-lambe* is the name given to colourful hand-set letterpress fly-posters that once covered the streets of São Paulo, advertising underground events. The name means "lick-lick" (referring to the way in which the posters are pasted on the walls), and Gráfica Fidalga is now the only workshop in Brazil that continues to produce these traditional woodblock-printed posters. By making books and prints, however, contemporary artists are reviving this dying craft and keeping the city streets vibrant, ensuring that Brazilian design continues to embrace and ravish the senses.

PREVIOUS PAGE
Copacabana tiles; "Pixo Gratis" *lambe-lambe* poster by Eltono.

ABOVE
The Manoel da Nóbrega Pavilion by Oscar Niemeyer.

Wish Casa

Country
Brazil

Work
**Identity
Publishing**

Capturing the spirit of Brazil's people and spaces, *Wish Casa* is a bold departure from previous lifestyle magazines. Answering the call to create a publication that the Brazilian market had never seen before, it provides an intimate look at the architecture, art and interiors that make the country so unique.

Winkreative's approach was to develop a distinctly personal magazine – a thoughtful look inside the homes, collections and spaces of fascinating individuals – which is reflected in the editorial content, the graphic design and the photography. Inspired by modernist architecture and furniture design, the look is structured and textured, with a bright colour palette and honest, un-retouched photography.

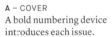
A – COVER
A bold numbering device introduces each issue.

A

WISH
— CASA

A – LOGO
With the bold sans serif font, focus is immediately drawn to "Casa", the heart of the magazine.

B – SYMBOL
The design plays with elements of houses and architecture.

C – NUMBERS
The *Wish Casa* numbering system was designed using the idea of building blocks.

D – ICONS
Symbols are used in the magazine to denote features such as "Botanics" and "City Tour".

E – COLOUR PALETTE
The colours are inspired by the vibrancy of the Brazilian lifestyle.

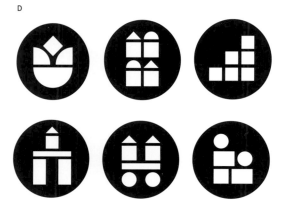

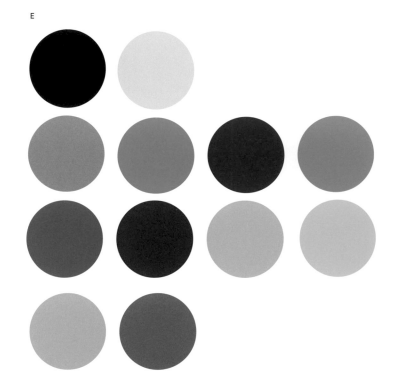

F – COVERS
The issue number is placed confidently on each cover to complement the playful photography.

G – SPREAD
Bright colours and symbols add Brazilian flair to editorial features.

PREVIOUS PAGES –
PHOTOGRAPHY

THIS PAGE, OPPOSITE
– SPREADS
The work of local
photographers and
the use of a vibrant
colour palette are
key to building the
definitive aesthetic
of the magazine.

URBE

Pacaembu e Higienópolis

Se meu prédio falasse

O paulistano é bairrista. Fato incontestável, até porque grandes deslocamentos são impossíveis por aqui. Moro no Pacaembu há 20 anos e há sete trouxe meu escritório dos Jardins para cá – questão de comodidade. Minha cidade é basicamente Higienópolis e Pacaembu. É a parte mais interessante, culta e politizada da metrópole. Uma extensão do Centro que deu certo.

Historicamente, esses bairros foram criados para atender a demanda da alta burguesia, mas nasceram de formas bem antagônicas. Em Higienópolis, os loteamentos foram feitos pelos alemães Martinho Buchard e Victor Nothmann, que planejaram um bairro de alto padrão para receber os barões do café e suas famílias, que migraram dos Campos Elíseos. Chamado de Boulevard Bouchard, o bairro foi lançado em 1895 e depois receberia o nome atual, Higienópolis, devido aos diferenciais como água e rede de esgoto, além de iluminação a gás e linhas de bondes. Com a crise de 1929, a elite perdeu muito dinheiro e ali começou a venda dos grandes casarões. Os amplos terrenos ganharam prédios e se iniciou, consequentemente, a verticalização do bairro.

Já o surgimento do Pacaembu se deu pela Companhia City, empresa inglesa que chegou a São Paulo em 1912 e foi responsável também pelo loteamento do Jardim América. Apesar da topografia destavorável, os engenheiros conseguiram criar um bairro modelo e trouxeram melhorias básicas consideradas inovadoras, como eletricidade e encanamento de água e esgoto.

A equipe desenhou os lotes, canalizou o Ribeirão Pacaembu (em 1922), drenou e aterrou áreas e inaugurou a avenida principal, já arborizada de ponta a ponta. O projeto dos ingleses, aprovado pela Prefeitura de São Paulo em 1925, priorizou ruas sinuosas, estabeleceu que as casas não poderiam ter mais de dez metros de altura e manteve terrenos espaçosos, com grandes áreas verdes. Hoje o bairro é um dos pulmões da cidade e a região continua intacta graças ao tombamento.

Aos poucos, o Pacaembu foi sendo ocupado por uma mistura sui generis: lá estavam os médicos, advogados, intelectuais – Sérgio Buarque de Hollanda e Guilherme de Almeida viveram ali durante décadas. Excelentes arquitetos contratados por famílias cultas e ascendentes puderam riscar seu traço naquela parte da Capital. Ainda hoje, caminhando pelas ruas arborizadas, podemos ver obras bem conservadas de Vilanova Artigas, Paulo Mendes da Rocha, Gregori Warchavchik, Fonseca Rodrigues e muitos outros.

Higienópolis teve um destino um pouco diferente: ainda é possível observar casarões desenhados por arquitetos como Carlos Ekman ou Victor Dubugras, mas o caráter atual do bairro formou-se a partir da década de 50, com edifícios projetados por grandes modernistas como Rino Levi, Vilanova Artigas e Artacho Jurado.

Andar pelas ruas de Higienópolis e do Pacaembu é um convite para se apreciar o melhor da arquitetura paulistana e, por que não, brasileira.

A seguir, destaco alguns deles:

Por Arthur Casas
Fotografias André Vieira

Arthur Casas percorre Pacaembu e Higienópolis e revela os segredos arquitetônicos dos bairros que se confundem e se complementam

URBE SE MEU PRÉDIO FALASSE

PACAEMBU E HIGIENÓPOLIS

A *Edifício Bretagne, 1958*
de João Artacho Jurado (1907–1983)

Jurado foi um arquiteto com grande apreço pelas linhas ornamentais, e ergueu neste endereço um edifício audacioso e muito interessante. Não que a sua arquitetura faça a minha cabeça, mas considero sim o Bretagne um projeto bem legal. No contexto em que foi construído, havia uma tendência de espaços decorativos, uma coisa meio Miami meio Los Angeles. Ele instalou ali uma grande infraestrutura, com piscina, bar, salão de jogos, sala de música e jardim na cobertura – algo bastante inovador para a época.

Av. Higienópolis, 938

B *Edifício Louveira, 1946*
de João Batista Vilanova Artigas (1915–1985)
e Carlos Cascaldi (1918–2010)

O prédio (na página anterior) é um ícone paulistano. O desnível interno foi uma grande novidade naquele final da década de 40, assim como o tamanho superdimensionado dos vãos de vidro e as passarelas, incríveis. O apartamento não é grande: tem três dormitórios. Mas o Louveira é prova viva de que Artigas foi um gigante.

Praça Vilebóin, esquina com a R. Piauí, Higienópolis

C *Edifício Dienz, 1957*
de Victor Reif (1909–1998)

Prédio amarelo de apartamentos pequenos, mas com homessidade perfeita – coisa rara em Higienópolis! A implantação é muito bacana, já que a construção foi armada longe do passeio público. É um edifício racionalista, simples, mas muito, muito bonito. Gosto do hall de entrada, arredondado, que contrasta com as linhas quadradas da fachada. Há ainda uma escultura de Domenico Calabrone na entrada, mosaico ajardinado e desenhos de Pietro Bardi no hall social.

R. Maranhão, 270, Higienópolis

D *Edifício Cinderela, 1956*
de João Artacho Jurado (1907–1983)

Com nome de princesa, o primeiro edifício do arquiteto assemelha-se com ares de palácio de fim de conto: revestimento de pastilhas bege e colunas em rosa e grandes sacadas com rebuscada gradil azuis. Na entrada, um imenso painel de mármore sustenta o nome do prédio. Na divisão do hall são detrás de repisa nas paredes vazadas, que formam o desenho de flores-de-lis.

R. Maranhão, 163, Higienópolis

"É a parte mais interessante, culta e politizada da metrópole. Uma extensão do Centro que deu certo"

SÃO PAULO

E *Edifício Lausanne, 1958*
de Adolf Franz Heep (1902–1378)

Adolf Franz Heep trabalhou com Le Corbusier na França e depois com Jacques Pilon, em São Paulo. Foi ele quem projetou o enorme edifício Itália, um dos ícones da cidade. O Lausanne tem uma característica bem legal, que são as cores da fachada, verde, vermelho e branco, que variam de apartamento para apartamento. Esses tons se alternam e deixam o prédio com um efeito bem bonito. O mural de pastilhas da entrada é outro leitor que chama a atenção.

Av. Higienópolis, 101

F *Casa Modernista, 1930*
de Gregori Warchavchik (1896–1972)

Um ícone modernista, mas de um modernismo quase tímido, mais de fachada do que de conceito. Warchavchik e seus amigos da época sacrificam a arquitetura brasileira. A inauguração, em 1930, contou com vista de Le Corbusier e exposição de obras de Tarsila do Amaral e Lasar Segall. Ano passado, a casa reabriu para visitação, em comemoração aos seus 80 anos. No site modernistablog.com tem vídeos com depoimento de arquitetos e artistas sobre a importância dessa que é uma das casas mais interessantes de São Paulo.

R. Itápolis, 961, Pacaembu

G *Casa Castró 202, 1937*
de Jayme Fonseca Rodrigues (1905–1946)

Uma casa incrível, feita para o próprio uso do arquiteto, que viveu muitos anos ali. Além de dela, Jayme desenhou todos os móveis, tudo art déco. É um exemplo da típica escola entre o déco e o modernismo. Hoje, a residência abriga o escritório de advocacia de Ernesto Tzirulnik, que levou dez anos para conseguir comprar o imóvel. Ele encantou-se com construção com onde o cuidado e usou até o recurso da mica, técnica de revestimento há muito esquecida pela arquitetura.

R. Gessé, 202, Pacaembu

H *Bretagne: personagens*

Moradores do Bretagne há cinco anos, a cantora e ex-VJ da MTV Madame Mim (alcunha artística de Mariana Eva) nasceu em Buenos Aires. Ela e o aplausívos pela extravagância do edifício. Foi amor à primeira vista. "Tenho certeza que um dos motivos de eu gostar tanto da cidade é morar neste lugar, com cara de clube. A história dos vizinhos é jovem: tem arquiteto, artista, jornalista. A gente se identifica", diz.

A

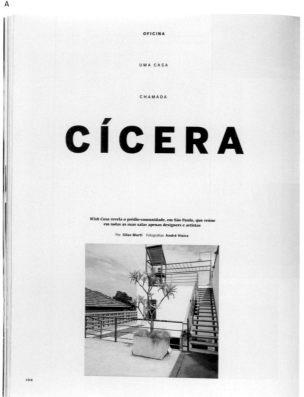

B

A – SPREAD
The "Cícera" feature offers an in depth look at local design talent.

B – MAP
The "City Tour" feature is supported by a commissioned map.

Craft and quality provide long-lasting solutions,
from a pencil sharpener to a landmark building.
Join us as we celebrate the art of making.

Projects
Mitsui Fudosan and Stanhope Plc
Andreas Martin-Löf Arkitekter | BlackBerry
Craft Design Technology

Client
Mitsui Fudosan and Stanhope Plc

Country
United Kingdom

Work
**Identity
Publishing
Digital design**

In the heart of London's Mayfair neighbourhood, 5 Hanover Square is a new mixed-use development. The striking, Georgian-inspired development comprises residential units, office space and an outpost of the esteemed international art gallery Blain|Southern. The building was developed by Mitsui Fudosan and Stanhope Plc and was designed by the architecture firm Squire and Partners.

Winkreative conceived a visual identity and produced a limited-run publication for the development, devising a simple logotype and a timeless black-on-black pattern for the branded materials. The publication, which includes essays by such prominent thinkers as the *Financial Times*'s architecture critic Edwin Heathcote and the English Heritage chief executive Simon Thurley, was printed with gilded edges, a subtle nod to the gold detailing on the building itself. To correspond with the project, Winkreative also designed and built a website.

A

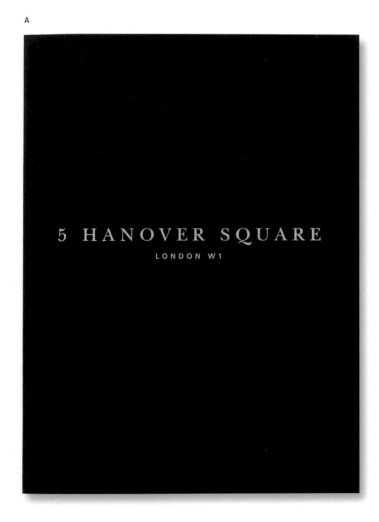

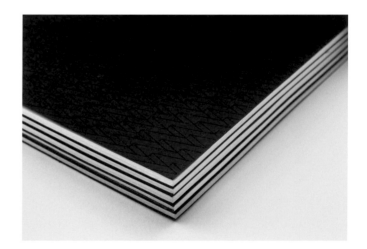

A – COVER
The Baskerville font dates back to the early 18th century when Hanover Square was founded. The cover has a subtle sawtooth texture, inspired by the building's roof design. The black in the colour palette draws from the unique black bricks, used in Georgian times.

5 Hanover Square
CONTACTS

MITSUI FUDOSAN (UK) LTD
7th Floor, Berger House
38 Berkeley Square
London W1J 5AE
Telephone: +44 (0)20 7318 4570
www.mitsuifudosan.co.uk

STANHOPE PLC
Norfolk House
31 St. James's Square
London SW1Y 4JJ
Telephone: +44 (0)20 7170 1700
www.stanhopeplc.com

CBRE
Henrietta House
Henrietta Place
London W1G 0NB
Telephone: +44 (0)20 7182 2000
www.cbre.com

DTZ
48 Warwick Street
London W1B 5NL
Telephone: +44 (0)20 3296 3000
www.dtz.com

DESIGN
Winkreative

PHOTOGRAPHY
Mark Sanders

ILLUSTRATIONS
Claire Rollet

PORTRAIT ILLUSTRATIONS
Henry Obasi

B – SPREADS
Winkreative challenged convention and commissioned illustrators, as opposed to renderers, to convey the vision of the completed building and the lifestyle it promises.

NEXT PAGES –
PHOTOGRAPHY
To champion the craftsmanship of the building, the materials were treated as iconic pieces and photographed accordingly. The Mayfair surroundings are photographed in a reportage style.

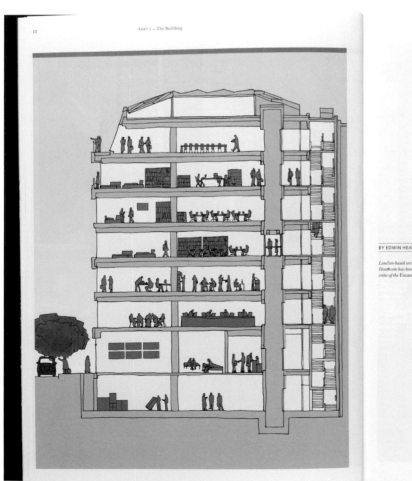

Living for the City:
A CASE FOR THE MODERN OFFICE

The digital era means that we're no longer chained to our desks, and the city itself has become our workplace. Still, the office matters today as much as ever.

BY EDWIN HEATHCOTE

London-based architect, designer and writer Edwin Heathcote has been the architecture and design critic of the Financial Times since 1999.

As connectivity increases, as we begin to work, communicate and exist in cyberspace, it is an intriguing paradox that real space – the city and the office itself – has become more crucial to the quality of our lives and our work.

The modernist age, predicated on the universality of the office, is dissolving. The concept of the office remains crucial – a critical component of the city – but it is no longer the core of commercial life; instead, the city itself has become the main stage for business. As smartphones and laptops allow the streets to become conduits of information and exchange, the civic sphere becomes as much of a workplace as the office.

In this vision, city and office form an integrated workplace. But for this vision to function, the metropolis needs to offer a particular cocktail of citiness, in which the most attractive elements of urban life are amplified. There are few better examples of this than Mayfair. Its discreet elegance, its blend of residential, retail and restaurants (the civic three 'R's), and its architectural character has created a profound sense of place. The global businesses that have settled here have done so because of that intensity of accumulated culture. Mayfair offers an increasingly urbane streetscape, encompassing extraordinary hotels and houses, some of the world's finest dining, and retail that's specific to a particular vision of Englishness. It is a streetscape that is a place to be.

But if the workplace becomes the city, what becomes of the office? What of architecture itself? The function of a building within a city is to become a component of urbanity.

Modernism proposed a zoned city in which work, play and sleep were separate, but the contemporary city is rediscovering a zoning in which buildings accommodate diverse uses. This banding of retail, commercial and residential ensures that the city is alive throughout the day. 5 Hanover Square facilitates this kind of non-stop, multifaceted urban life, balancing office space with a ground-level art gallery and residential units.

The contemporary office also needs to function as an extension of a public realm. Certainly the desks, the views and the natural light are crucial but even more so is the communal space. Offices today exist primarily because people like to be together; they enjoy each other's company. Thus it is the communal spaces – lobbies, stairs, meeting rooms and lifts – that become the sites of real communication and of serendipitous meeting, as the office becomes a mini-metropolis.

5 Hanover Square achieves this, and it also learns from London's ultimate architectural archetype: the flat-fronted Georgian house. This restrained, neutral, adaptable and flexible building speaks of where it is; it is about the intensification and continuation of a real place. As workers live in an increasingly virtual world, the genius loci, the sense of the particular within a real space, becomes pivotal, and architecture is at the heart of a building's sense of place. 5 Hanover Square, sited in the heart of Mayfair, London's most successfully urbane centre, offers this sense of place. It is a building for workers, for artists, for citizens – but most of all, it is a building for the city.

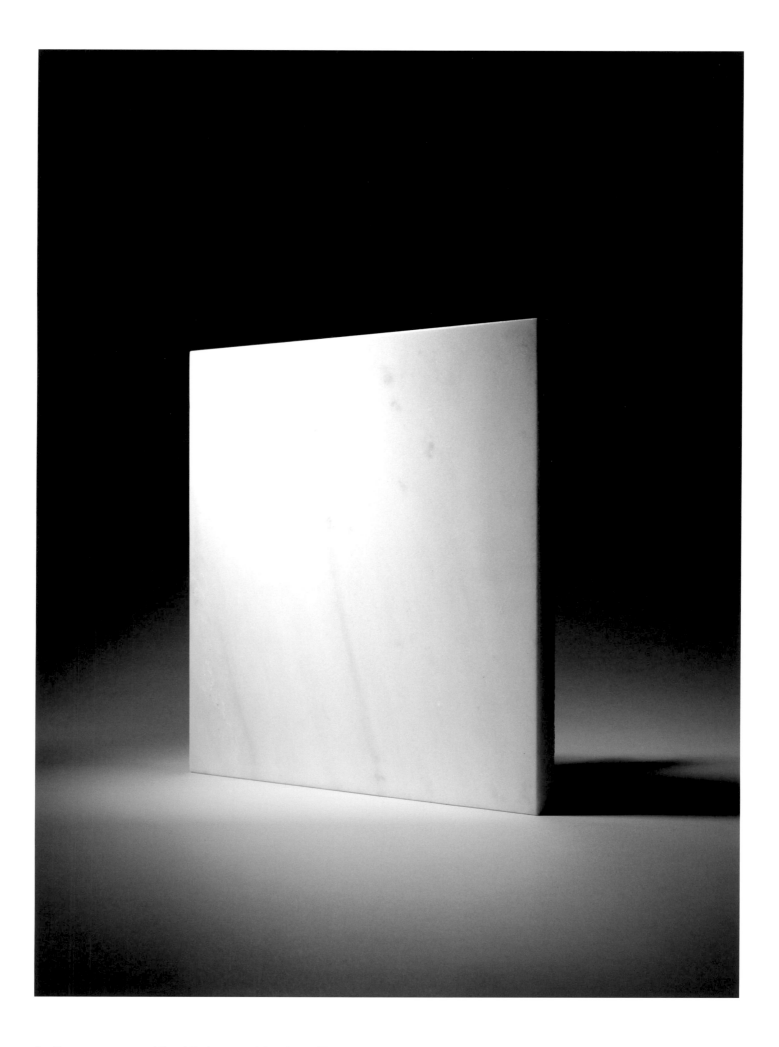

Client
Andreas Martin-Löf Arkitekter

Country
Sweden

Work
Identity

Winkreative worked with Andreas Martin-Löf Arkitekter in the early days of the practice. As the practice grew, it needed an identity to reflect its dynamism and vigour and the gravitas of a reputable, established firm.

In addition to architectural projects, the practice designs products, exhibition installations and interiors, so Winkreative created a bold, simple logotype and marque that are flexible enough to work across a range of applications. In embossed copper foil, the marque communicates timelessness.

The firm went on to refurbish Midori House, Winkreative's London headquarters in leafy Marylebone.

A

ANDREAS MARTIN-LÖF ARKITEKTER

B

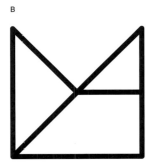

A – LOGO
The classic modernist typeface and monogram are both contemporary and practical, echoing the firm's hands-on approach.

B – SYMBOL
The marque suggests the elements of building and making structures.

A – STATIONERY
Natural brown papers,
industrial ring-bound
notepads and simply
crafted closing
techniques reflect a
functional and honest
approach to architecture.

ANDREAS MARTIN-LÖF
ARKITEKTER

BJURHOLMSGATAN 7A, 116 38 STOCKHOLM
+46 8 644 77 02 · OFFICE@MARTINLOF.SE
WWW.MARTINLOF.SE

Winkreative
1 Dorset Street
London W1U 4EG
United Kingdom

12 May 2011

Dear Winkreative

Founded in
projects
abro

Client
BlackBerry

Country
Canada

Work
**Publishing
Advertising
Environment**

In anticipation of the launch of BlackBerry's PlayBook, Winkreative devised a series of collaborations with leading accessories designers to create a collection of superior cases for the tablet. Selected brands include fine artisans such as Brooklyn, Delvaux, Ettinger, Porter, Valextra and WANT Les Essentiels de la Vie, with each revealing a different aesthetic but sharing a commitment to quality.

Winkreative photographed the collection, producing a print advertising campaign and a special insert, which was distributed with

copies of *Monocle* magazine. The agency also hosted lively launch events in London and New York.

A previous project with BlackBerry was *Hive* magazine, an internal publication distributed at BlackBerry to keep its team abreast of key global design trends and influences. It was conceived by Winkreative to be the voice of BlackBerry's industrial design team, and each issue is dedicated to a country and includes features, brand collaborations and profiles of design greats.

A

A, B – PRINT CAMPAIGN
The promotional photography for the launch of the Made for PlayBook collection combines state-of-the-art technology with handcrafted materials. Carefully chosen props allude to the craftsmanship of the cases, and bold colours bring it to life. The print insert was distributed with copies of *Monocle* magazine as well as at the launch event.

NEXT PAGES–
ADVERTISING
The BlackBerry is seamlessly integrated into all aspects of a contemporary lifestyle.

PATTERN
Bespoke patterns were designed for use as screen savers.

BlackBerry   Craft

A

AMADANA
DESIGNS

By Danielle Demetriou

For the man behind Amadana, the Japanese design company responsible for the nation's sleekest home appliances and electronic devices, the quest for the perfect design recipe is an important one.

HIVE — BlackBerry Global Design Briefing

14 – 15

PREVIOUS PAGES –
ADVERTISING
Connected and comfortable: the discreet placement of the BlackBerry within the scene suggests that users can stay connected even from the peaceful surroundings of a Rocky Mountain lodge. The BlackBerry sits naturally among the other design objects in the space.

A – SPREADS
Product design is given particular emphasis in *Hive*.

B – COVERS
Each issue of the magazine is dedicated to a country, and each vibrant screen-printed dust jacket is colour co-ordinated to match the hue chosen to represent the country.

B

Client
**Craft Design
Technology**

Country
Japan

Work
**Identity
Packaging**

"Three Words, One World" is the mission statement behind the stationery company Craft Design Technology. Combining modern design with traditional Japanese craft and technological innovation, Craft Design Technology instills exceptional design quality into essential everyday objects.

Winkreative provided creative direction across all aspects of the business, including brand name, logo and overall corporate identity. The website, brand promotional material and accompanying photography were informed by a design aesthetic that celebrates a contemporary lifestyle influenced by heritage.

A

Craft Design Technology™

クラフト
デザイン
テクノロジー

A – IDENTITY
The corporate identity features two distinct logos: one in English, made up of a traditional serif typeface; and a second, smaller mark, with accompanying Japanese text. This was influenced by Japanese postmarks and family crests and was intentionally designed as a small-usage mark, required to brand stationery items.

NEXT PAGES –
PHOTOGRAPHY, PRODUCT DESIGN
Bespoke resin shelves were made featuring laser-cut logos. The entire collection was arranged so that a recognisable home office stationery and storage system could be understood. The packaging system was included to complete the branding story.

Designed by the Japan-based architecture and product design firm Intentionallies, the products were informed by the Mingei craft movement in Japan, to make the simplest everyday item the most beautiful. Winkreative contributed graphic-design services to their vision for the new stationery. Materials such as brass, leather, handmade paper and bamboo were used to create a warm range that feels personal and refined. Colours and patterns were drawn directly from the Japanese landscape.

Craft Design Technology™

Craft Design Technology™

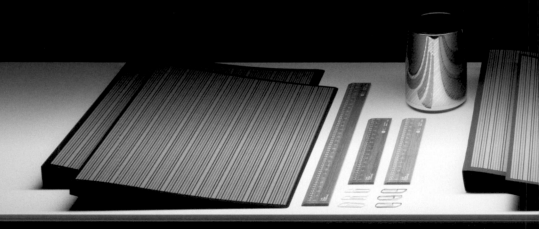

Craft Design Technology

People
and Process

**Photography by Daisuke Hamada
and Heiko Prigge**

The word *midori* means "green" in Japanese, reflecting
the balanced aesthetic and leafy outlook of Winkreative's
London design studio, Midori House. Above: design
leaders Corinna Drossel and Maurus Fraser.

Opposite page, clockwise from top left: Ariane Elfen; resident illustrator Erica Dorn works on Miles, a character in *The MINI International* magazine; Sabine Vandenbroucke. This page, from top: project team Emma Baines, Matt Adams, Simon Chong and Flora King; Corinna Drossel and Maurus Fraser.

Opposite page: Steve Teruggi. This page, from top:
Alexios Seilopoulos and Raphael Güller have lunch in the
garden; Ariel Childs and Joel Todd.

This page, from top: second floor, Midori House;
Adam Thompson and Atsushi Okahashi. Opposite page,
clockwise from top left: Ayako Terashima
and Raphael Güller; Clare Aitken.

This page, from top: Camila Bossolan;
Silke Klinnert and Hank Park.

Above, from left: Matthew Lowe, Leslie Kwok and Atsushi Okahashi. Below: product designer Shin Mononobe prepares packaging samples. Opposite: Tyler Brûlé.

Above, from top: Jennifer McAlear and Selina Pavel;
life on the second floor, Midori House; Simon Chong
and Maurus Fraser.

10 Key Moments

An illustrated journey through the past, present
and future of Winkreative

Illustrated by Keiko Nagano

1.
The birth of Winkreative

Exposed to an extraordinary amount of creative output from
around the globe, *Wallpaper* editor Tyler Brûlé has a eureka
moment that leads to a new type of editorial-driven agency.

2.
Shooting in the desert

In the early days of branded content, Camel cigarettes pulls in
"lifestyle guru" Tyler Brûlé and his team of three to create a
premium magazine. Luckily, in those days, we all smoked...

The turning point

The next step from magazines? An entire brand. In a buccaneer
moment, Tyler Brûlé gathers a team and goes for it. Swiss
International Air Lines relaunches, turning this annex of *Wallpaper*
into an independent agency that punches above its weight.

4.
Experience is everything

As a journalist, Tyler Brûlé believes in getting out, meeting people and seeing things first-hand. As Winkreative grows, creative cultural exposure swiftly follows, fondly becoming known as the "office inspiration trips".

5.
The Desk

Winkreative's first foray into multimedia, "The Desk" is a series of
mini global adventures. Producing content, title sequences, sound
and graphics for the BBC series, Winkreative establishes
a capability for the creation of film and animated content.

6.
Challenging conventions

Selling a sophisticated Canadian airline on the idea of using Toronto's biggest pest as a brand mascot is a challenge. Receiving mixed responses, the charming Mr. Porter becomes the successful face of Porter Airlines.

Day to night

World food Fridays: to sate the international appetites of
Winkreative's food fanatics, Midori House hosts luncheons
of Lebanese street food and Japanese okonomiyaki, as well
as German sausage feasts.

The family that eats and sings together stays together. Tyler Brûlé's
favourite karaoke song? "From Russia with Love".

8.

Winkreative goes global

It all starts in Zurich. The London design studio
comes next, followed by New York, Tokyo, Hong Kong
and Toronto.

9.
The quest for the perfect tote

Because everyone needs a good tote bag. Somewhat of an obsession at Midori House and fuelled by our hunger for all things print, our global search for something sturdy and stylish continues.

10.
Design stories

With a current portfolio of 45 active clients and 50 staff, we turn
the spotlight on ourselves – the toughest client of all.

Here's to 15 years of telling stories
and all that the next 15 may hold.

Acknowledgements

MACH Architektur
Ingela P Arrhenius
Sandra Ban
Ralf Barthelmes
Russell Bell
Duarte Belo
Jo Bird
Joakim Blockstrom
Christian Borstlap
Lars Botten
Lorne Bridgman
Thomas Brown
Felix Brüggemann
Graham Clayton-Chance
Jordan Copeland
Despina Curtis
Kevin Dart
Luc Delahaye
Erica Dorn
Michael Edwards

Daniel Ehrenworth
Leandro Farina
Billy Farrell
Malika Favre
Bella Fenning
Romulo Fialdini
Dermot Flynn
Adrian Gaut
Neil Gardiner
GetStock/
Toronto Star
Christopher Griffith
Pedro Guimarães
Thomas Heinser
Mariano Herrera
Jason Hindley
Bill Hollyman
Richie Hopson
Robert Huber
Intentionallies
Shinichi Ito

Clement Jolin
Theodore Kaye
Letman
Will Lew
Ionic Shipping Ltd
Sebastian Lucrecio
Michael Magee
Eamon MacMahon
Izumi Masatoshi
Kasako Masunouchi
Iain McIntosh
Todd McLellan
Lotta Nieminen
Louisa Parry
Parko Polo
Heiko Prigge
Nexus Productions
Metz + Racine
The Quiet Revolution
Daniel Riera
Rinzen

Claire Rollet
Grischa Rüschendorf
Vesa Sammalisto
Graham Samuels
Mark Sanders
Beat Schweizer
Hoysoya Schaefer
Dan Tobin Smith
Dianna Snape
Jake Strangel
Kohei Take
Ruy Teixeira
Taro Terasawa
Jørn Tomter
Simon Upton
Paul Wetherell
Greg White
Christopher Wise
Wonderwall
Masao Yamazaki

Editorial team

EDITOR
Camilla Belton

ART DIRECTOR
Corinna Drossel

DESIGNER
Selina Pavel

PRODUCTION
Emma Baines
Nicola Applegate
Jacqueline Deacon
Jennifer McAlear

Winkreative management

CHAIRMAN, CEO
Tyler Brûlé

CFO
Sabine Vandenbroucke

MANAGING DIRECTOR
Ariel Childs

CREATIVE DIRECTOR
Maurus Fraser

STRATEGY DIRECTOR
Steve Teruggi

Thank you to all
Winkreative staff
past and present